ACOUSTIC MASTERS

CAT STEVENS

Wise Publications
8/9 Frith Street, London W1D 3JB, England.

Exclusive Distributors:
Music Sales Limited
Distribution Centre, Newmarket Road, Bury St. Edmunds, Suffolk IP33 3YB, England.
Music Sales Corporation
257 Park Avenue South, New York, NY10010, United States of America.
Music Sales Pty Limited
120 Rothschild Avenue, Rosebery, NSW 2018, Australia.

Order No. AM91350
ISBN 0-7119-3607-2
This book © Copyright 2003 by Wise Publications.

Cover designed by Fresh Lemon.
Music arranged by Martin Shellard and Arthur Dick.
Music processed by Paul Ewers Music Design and Jon Paxman.
Cover photograph by courtesy of Neal Preston/Corbis.
Compiled by Nick Crispin.
Printed in Malta by Interprint Limited.

Also available:

Acoustic Masters for Guitar: David Gray
Eighteen great acoustic guitar titles (Order No. AM944340)

Acoustic Masters for Guitar: Paul Simon
Eighteen great acoustic guitar titles (Order No. PS11572)

WISE PUBLICATIONS
part of The Music Sales Group
London / New York / Paris / Sydney / Copenhagen / Berlin / Madrid / Tokyo

CONTENTS

GUITAR TABLATURE EXPLAINED

Guitar music can be notated three different ways: on a musical stave, in tablature, and in rhythm slashes.

RHYTHM SLASHES are written above the stave. Strum chords in the rhythm indicated. Round noteheads indicate single notes.

THE MUSICAL STAVE shows pitches and rhythms and is divided by lines into bars. Pitches are named after the first seven letters of the alphabet.

TABLATURE graphically represents the guitar fingerboard. Each horizontal line represents a string, and each number represents a fret.

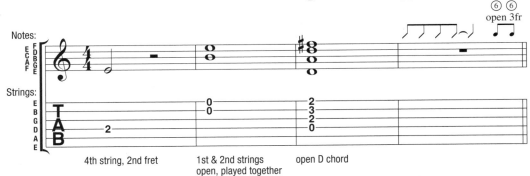

4th string, 2nd fret | 1st & 2nd strings open, played together | open D chord

DEFINITIONS FOR SPECIAL GUITAR NOTATION

SEMI-TONE BEND: Strike the note and bend up a semi-tone (1/2 step).

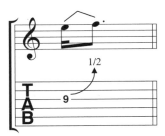

WHOLE-TONE BEND: Strike the note and bend up a whole-tone (whole step).

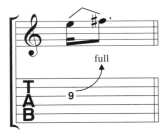

GRACE NOTE BEND: Strike the note and bend as indicated. Play the first note as quickly as possible.

QUARTER-TONE BEND: Strike the note and bend up a 1/4 step.

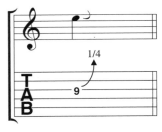

BEND & RELEASE: Strike the note and bend up as indicated, then release back to the original note.

COMPOUND BEND & RELEASE: Strike the note and bend up and down in the rhythm indicated.

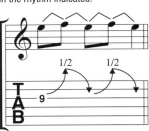

PRE-BEND: Bend the note as indicated, then strike it.

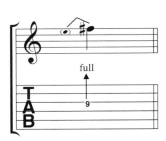

PRE-BEND & RELEASE: Bend the note as indicated. Strike it and release the note back to the original pitch.

UNISON BEND: Strike the two notes simultaneously and bend the lower note up to the pitch of the higher.

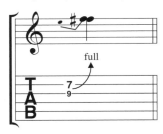

BEND & RESTRIKE: Strike the note and bend as indicated then restrike the string where the symbol occurs.

BEND, HOLD AND RELEASE: Same as bend and release but hold the bend for the duration of the tie.

BEND AND TAP: Bend the note as indicated and tap the higher fret while still holding the bend.

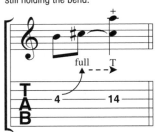

VIBRATO: The string is vibrated by rapidly bending and releasing the note with the fretting hand.

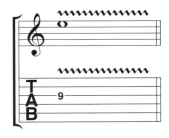

HAMMER-ON: Strike the first note with one finger, then sound the second note (on the same string) with another finger by fretting it without picking.

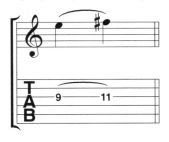

PULL-OFF: Place both fingers on the notes to be sounded, strike the first note and without picking, pull the finger off to sound the second note.

LEGATO SLIDE (GLISS): Strike the first note and then slide the same fret-hand finger up or down to the second note. The second note is not struck.

SHIFT SLIDE (GLISS & RESTRIKE): Same as legato slide, except the second note is struck.

MUFFLED STRINGS: A percussive sound is produced by laying the fret hand across the string(s) without depressing, and striking them with the pick hand.

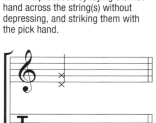

PALM MUTING: The note is partially muted by the pick hand lightly touching the string(s) just before the bridge.

SWEEP PICKING: Rhythmic downstroke and/or upstroke motion across the strings.

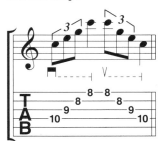

TRILL: Very rapidly alternate between the notes indicated by continuously hammering on and pulling off.

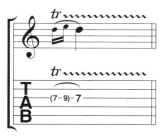

NATURAL HARMONIC: Strike the note while the fret-hand lightly touches the string directly over the fret indicated.

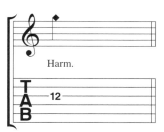

RAKE: Drag the pick across the strings indicated with a single motion.

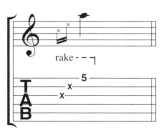

VIBRATO DIVE BAR AND RETURN: The pitch of the note or chord is dropped a specific number of steps (in rhythm) then returned to the original pitch.

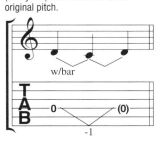

TAPPING: Hammer ("tap") the fret indicated with the pick-hand index or middle finger and pull off to the note fretted by the fret hand.

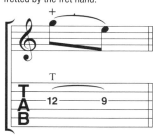

PINCH HARMONIC: The note is fretted normally and a harmonic is produced by adding the edge of the thumb or the tip of the index finger of the pick hand to the normal pick attack.

TREMOLO PICKING: The note is picked as rapidly and continuously as possible.

VIBRATO BAR SCOOP: Depress the bar just before striking the note, then quickly release the bar.

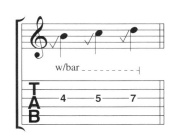

PICK SCRAPE: The edge of the pick is rubbed down (or up) the string, producing a scratchy sound.

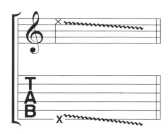

HARP HARMONIC: The note is fretted normally and a harmonic is produced by gently resting the pick hand's index finger directly above the indicated fret (in brackets) while plucking the appropriate string.

ARPEGGIATE: Play the notes of the chord indicated by quickly rolling them from bottom to top.

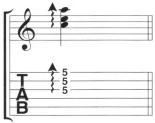

VIBRATO BAR DIP: Strike the note and then immediately drop a specific number of steps, then release back to the original pitch.

ADDITIONAL MUSICAL DEFINITIONS

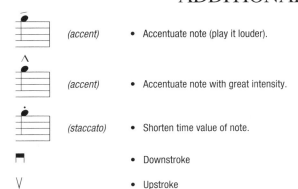

(accent) • Accentuate note (play it louder).

(accent) • Accentuate note with great intensity.

(staccato) • Shorten time value of note.

• Downstroke

∨ • Upstroke

NOTE: Tablature numbers in brackets mean:
1. The note is sustained, but a new articulation (such as hammer on or slide) begins.
2. A note may be fretted but not necessarily played.

D.%. al Coda

D.C. al Fine

tacet

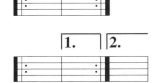

• Go back to the sign (%), then play until the bar marked *To Coda* ⊕ then skip to the section marked ⊕ *Coda*.

• Go back to the beginning of the song and play until the bar marked *Fine*.

• Instrument is silent (drops out).

• Repeat bars between signs.

• When a repeated section has different endings, play the first ending only the first time and the second ending only the second time.

THE BOY WITH A MOON & STAR ON HIS HEAD

WORDS & MUSIC BY CAT STEVENS

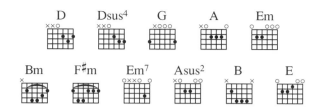

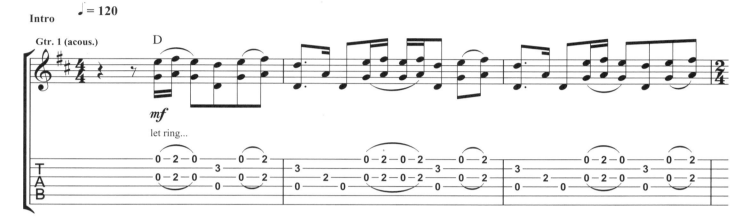

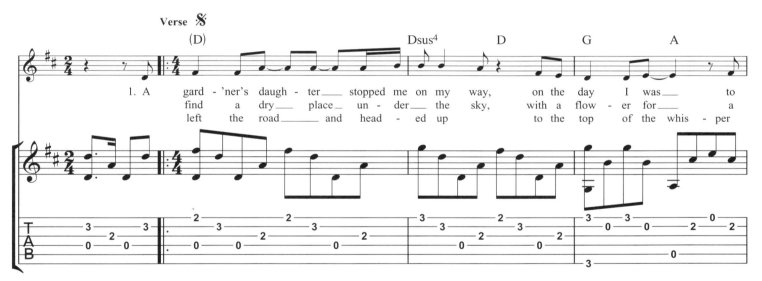

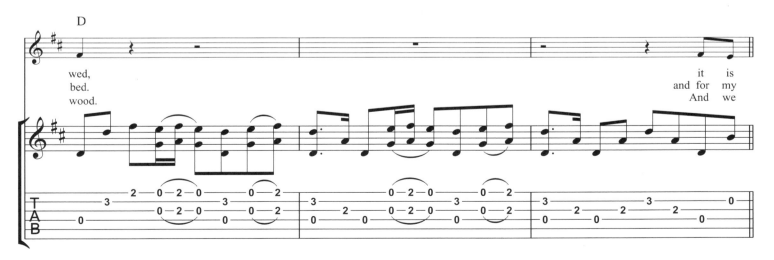

Chorus

you who I wish to share_ my bo - dy with, she
joy I will give you a boy with a
walked 'til we came to where_ the ho - ly mag - no - - - lia

said. 2. We'll
stood. 5. And

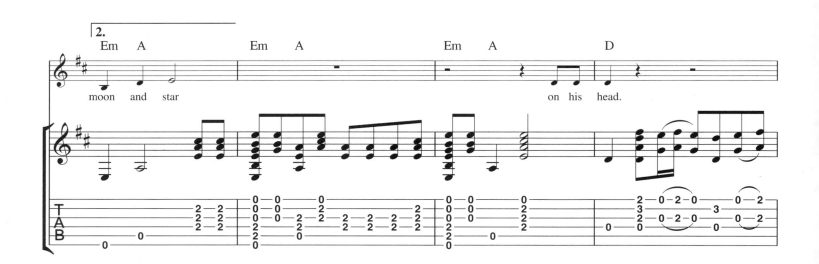

moon and star on his head.

3. Her

Verse

sil - ver hair___ flowed___ in the air, lay - ing waves ac - ross___ the sun.___

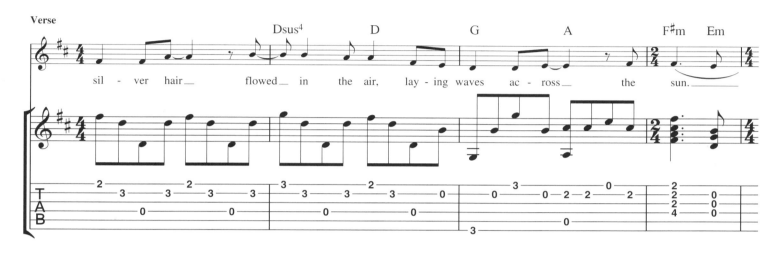

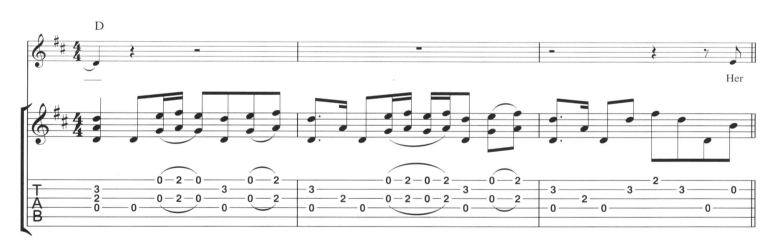

Her

Chorus

hands were like the white___ sands and her eyes___ had dia - monds

9

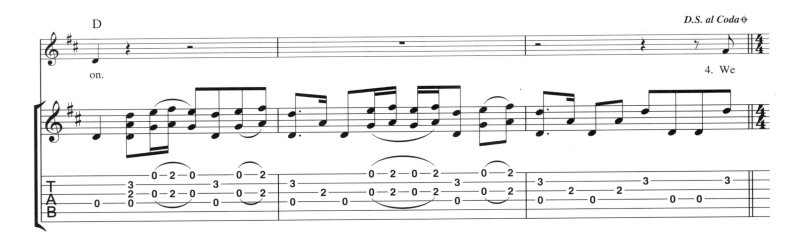

on.

4. We

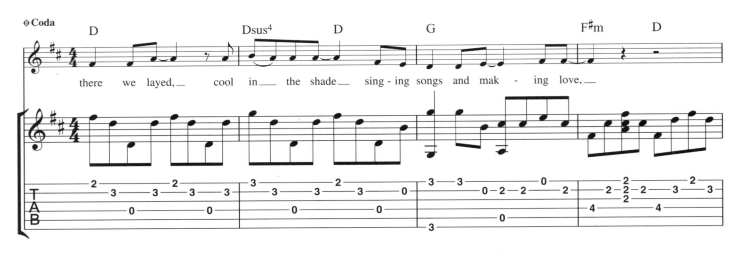

Coda

D   Dsus⁴   D   G   F♯m   D

there   we   layed,__   cool   in__   the   shade__   sing - ing   songs   and   mak - ing   love,__

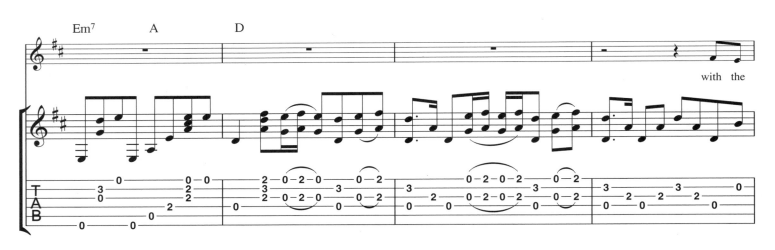

Em⁷   A   D

with   the

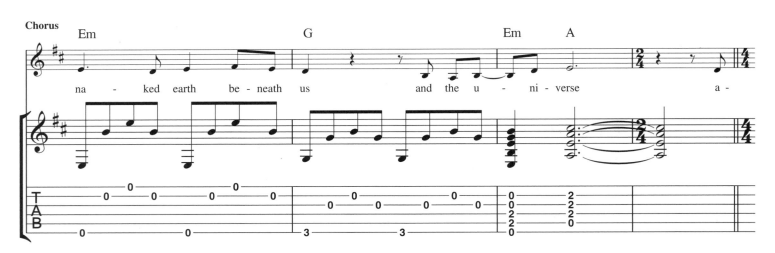

Chorus

Em   G   Em   A

na - ked   earth   be - neath   us   and   the   u - ni - verse   a -

10

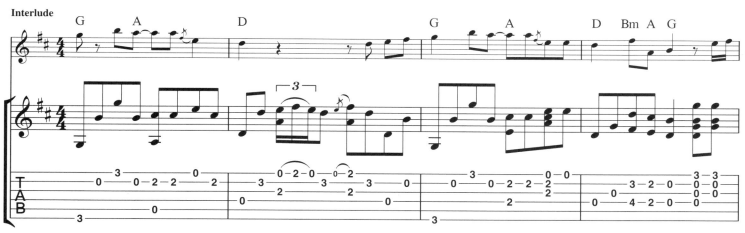

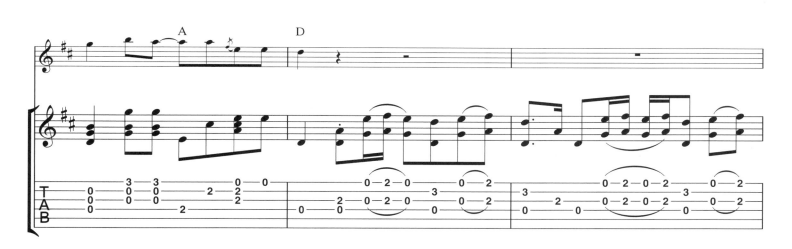

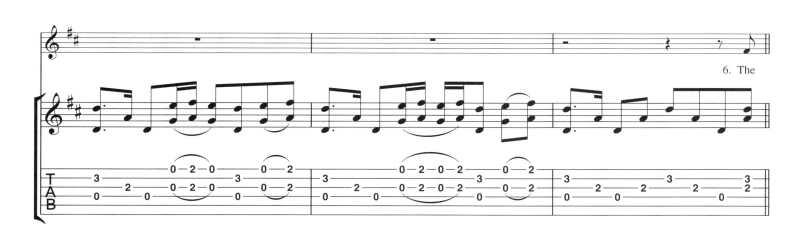

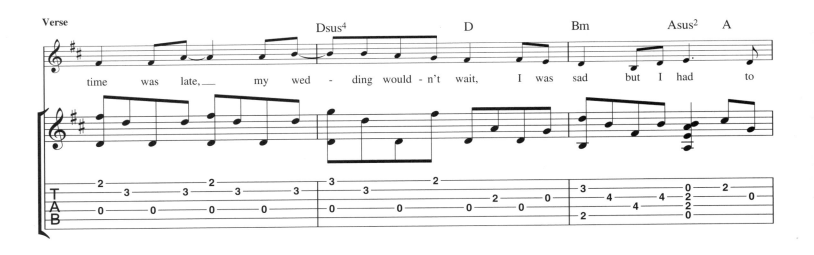

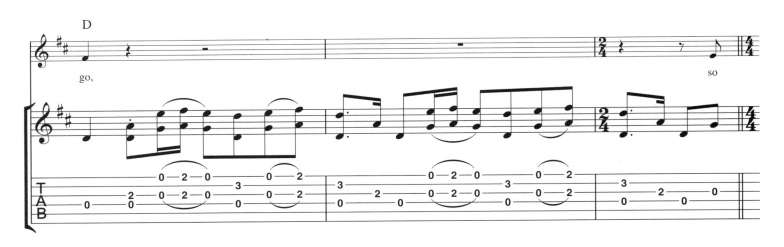

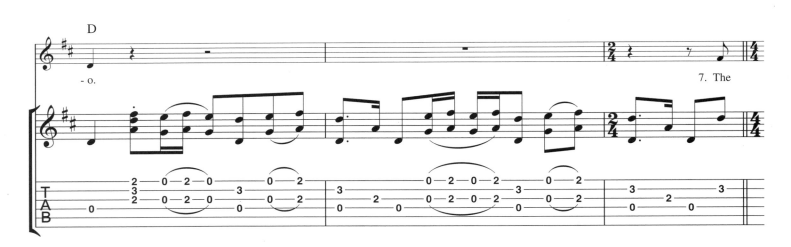

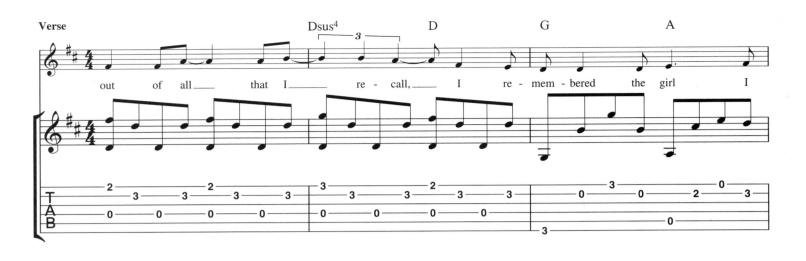

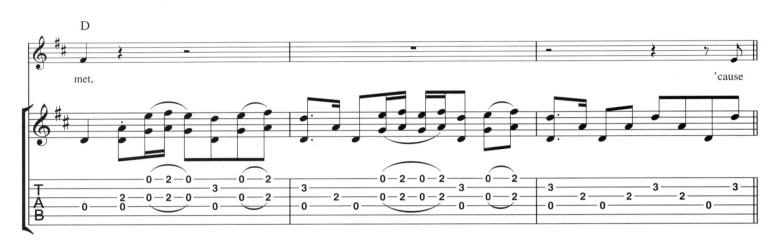

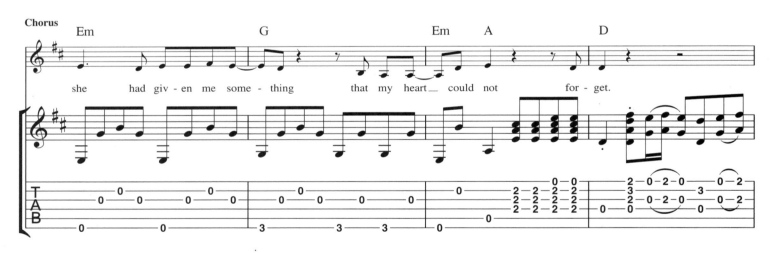

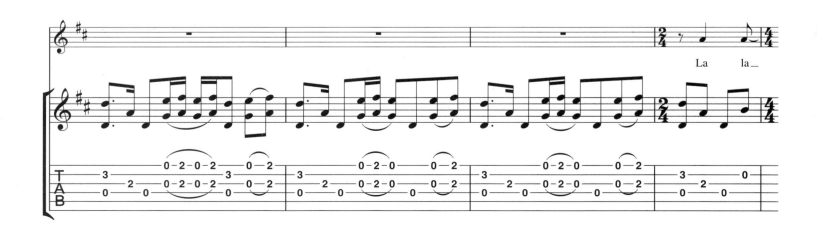

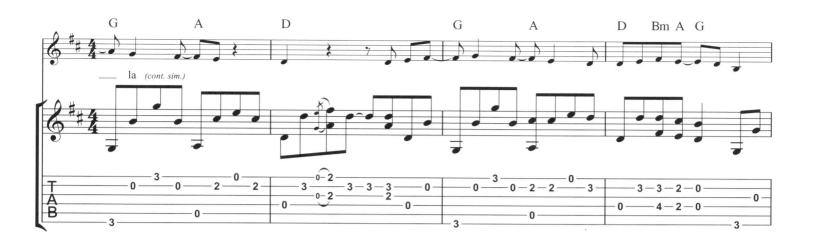

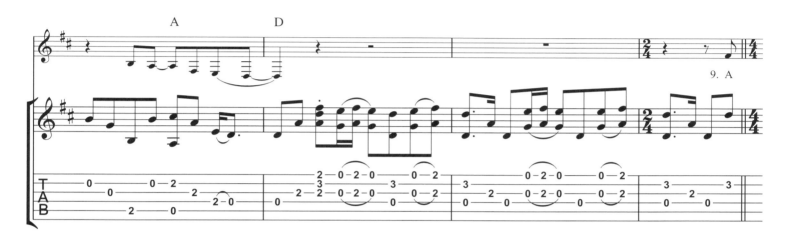

Verse

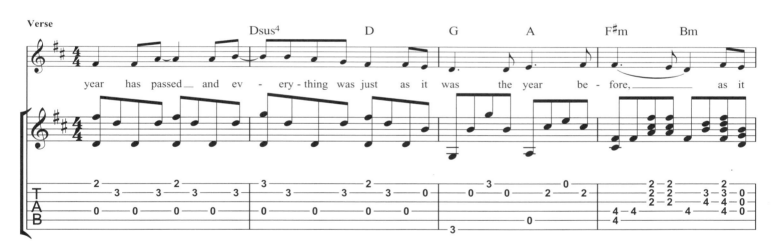

year has passed— and ev-ery-thing was just as it was the year be-fore,_____ as it

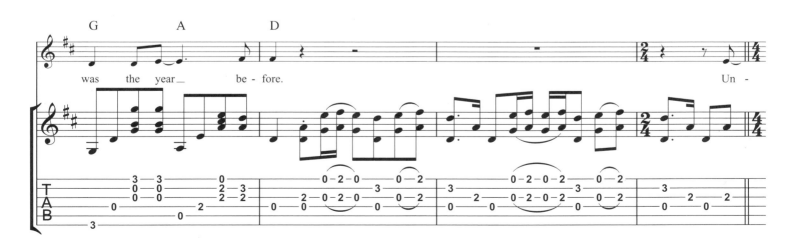

was the year_ be-fore. Un -

15

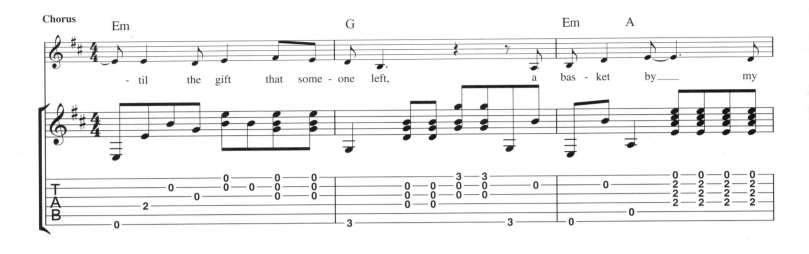

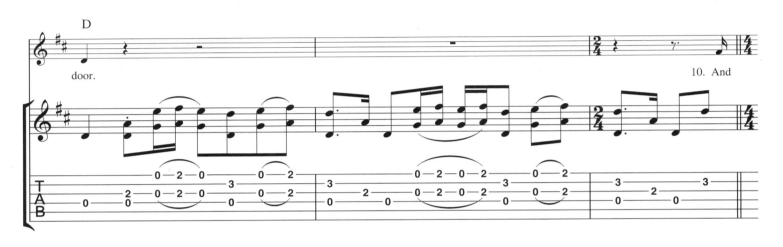

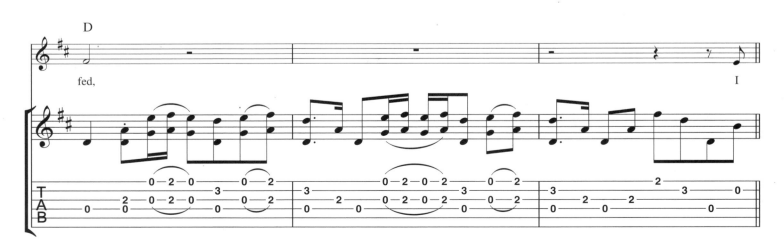

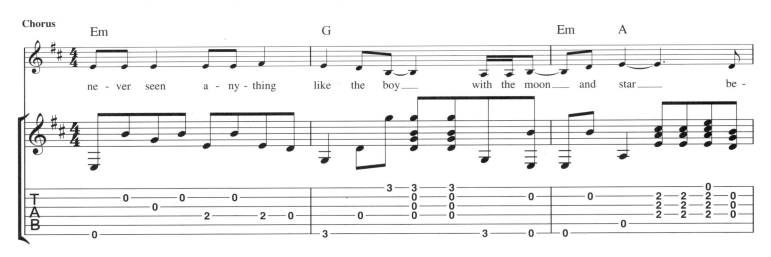

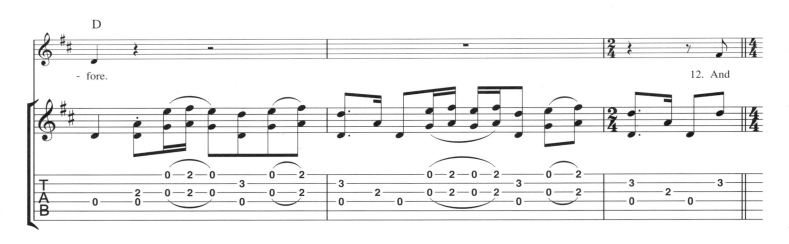

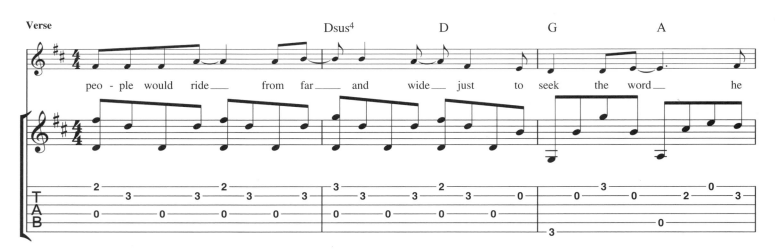

CAN'T KEEP IT IN

WORDS & MUSIC BY CAT STEVENS

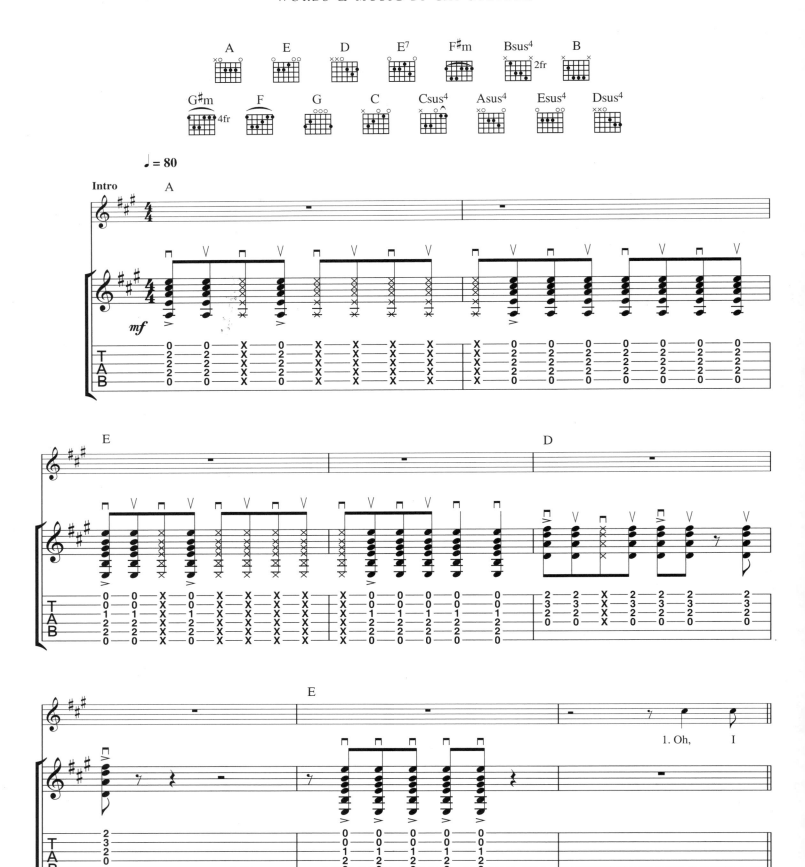

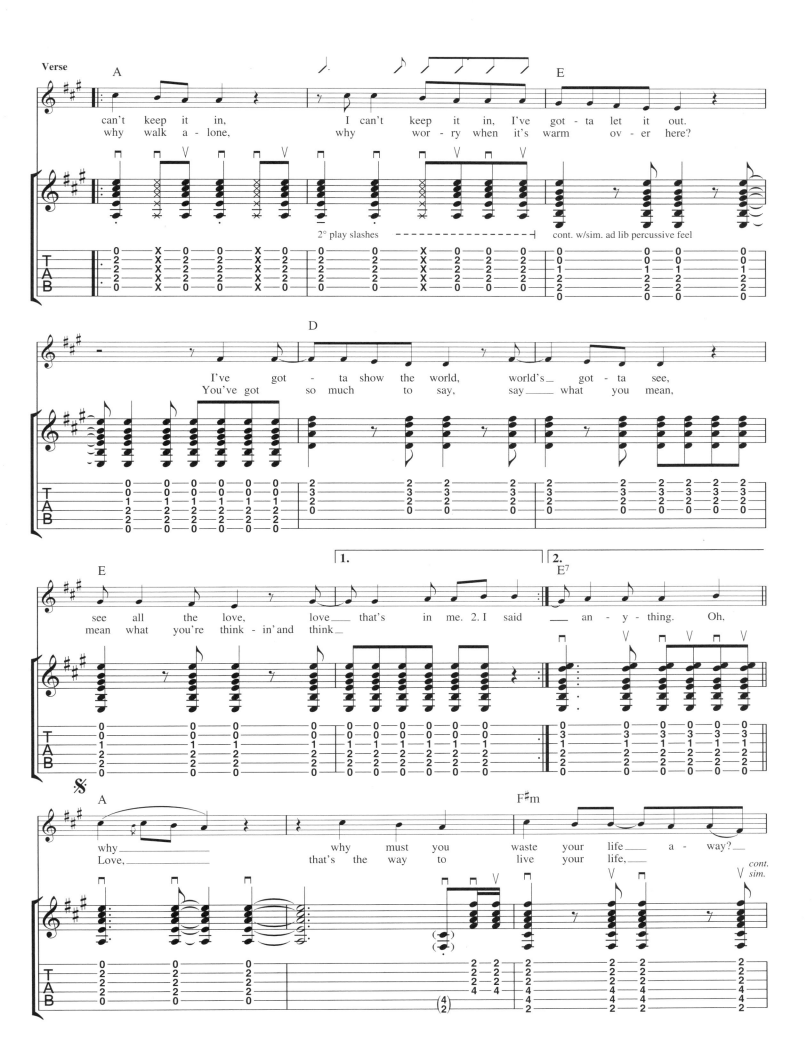

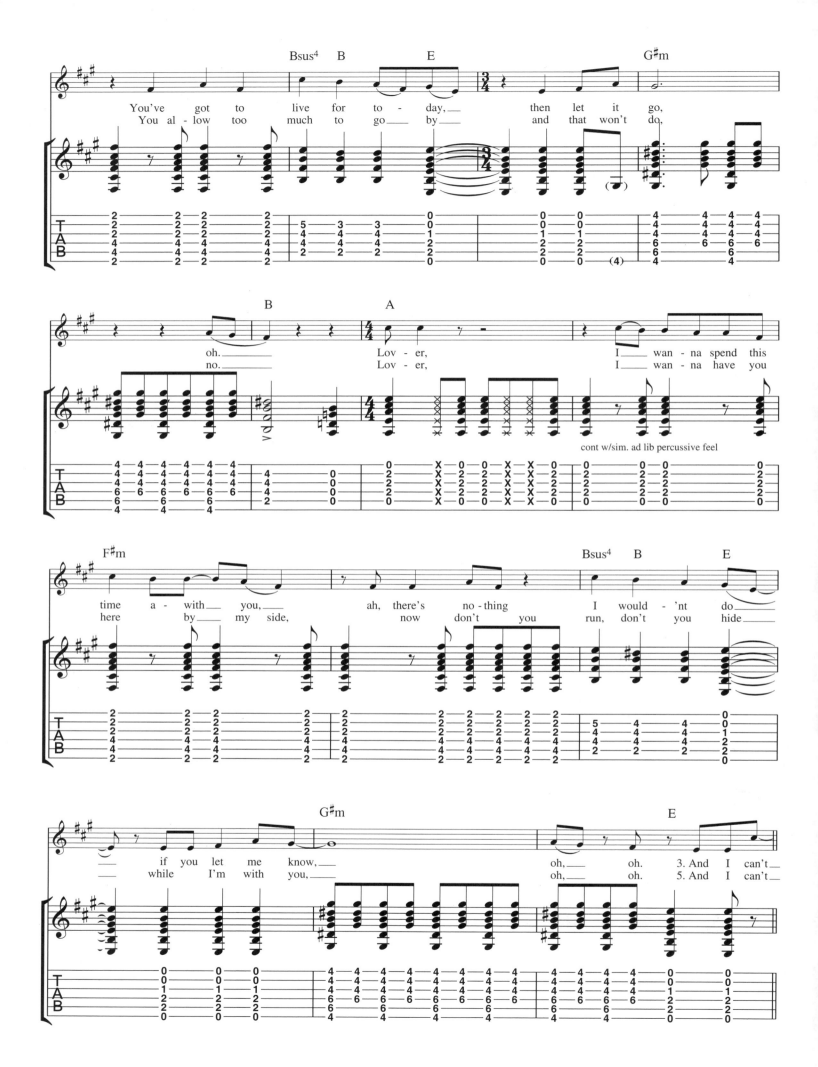

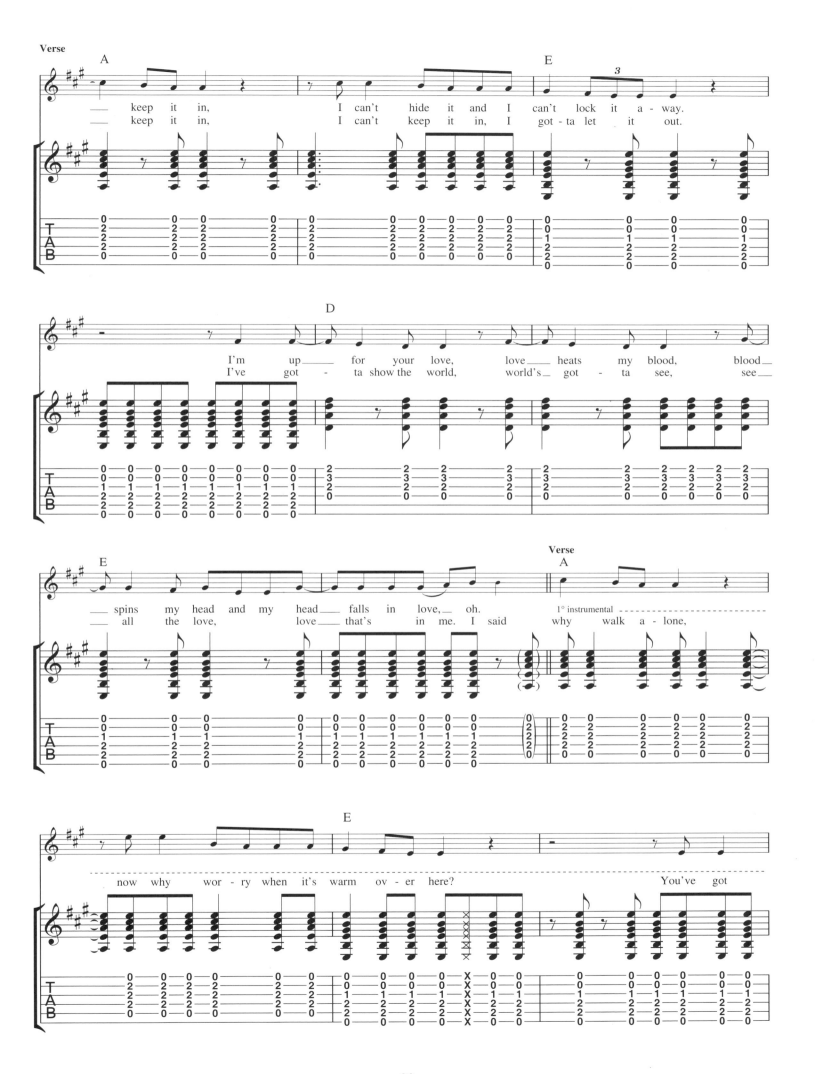

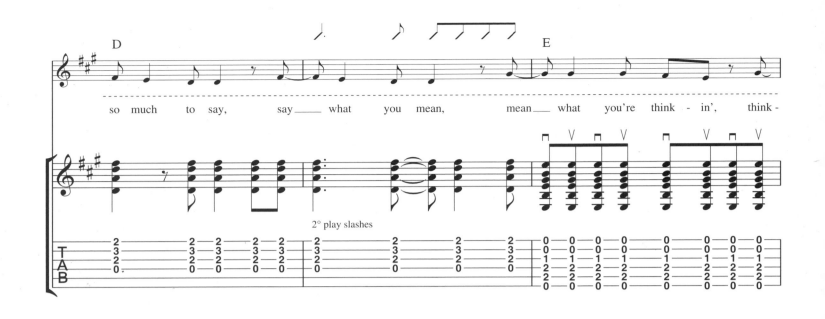

so much to say, say___ what you mean, mean___ what you're think - in', think -

2° play slashes

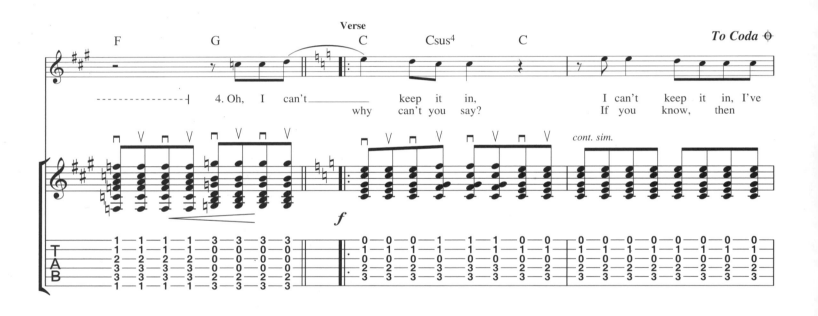

Verse

To Coda ⊕

4. Oh, I can't___ keep it in, I can't keep it in, I've
why can't you say? If you know, then

cont. sim.

f

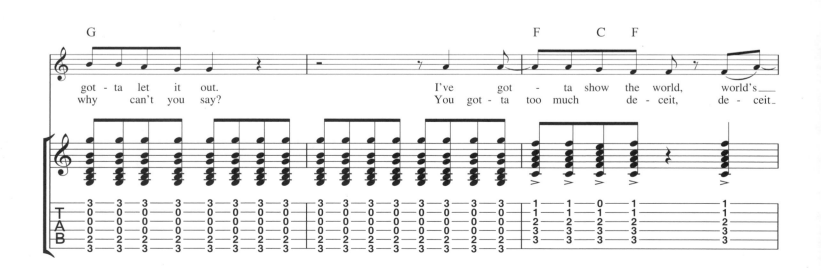

got - ta let it out. I've got - ta show the world, world's___
why can't you say? You got - ta too much de - ceit, de - ceit___

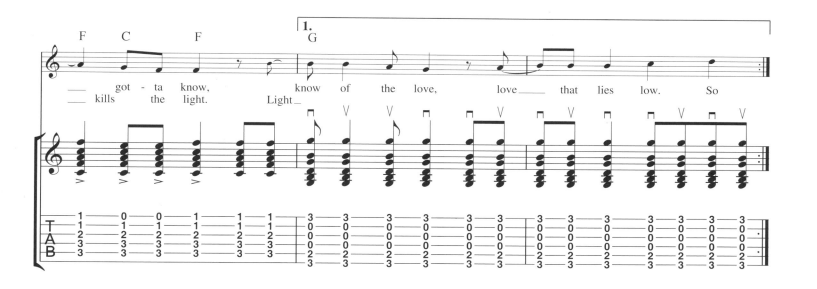

got - ta know, know of the love, love___ that lies low. So
kills the light. Light___

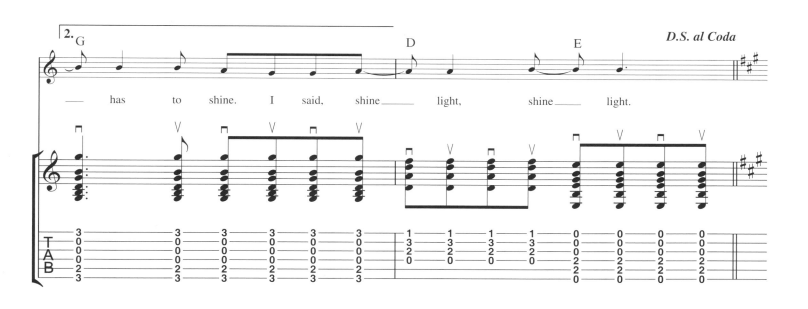

D.S. al Coda

has to shine. I said, shine___ light, shine___ light.

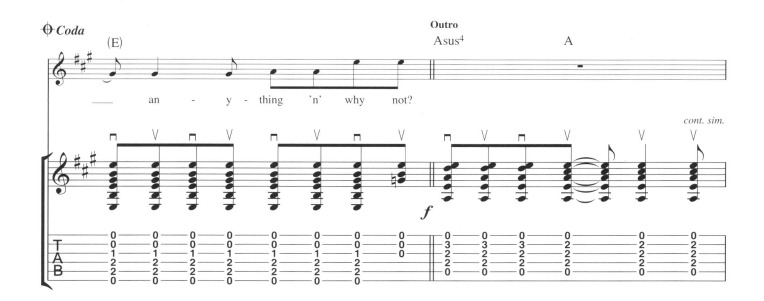

Coda

Outro

an - y - thing 'n' why not?

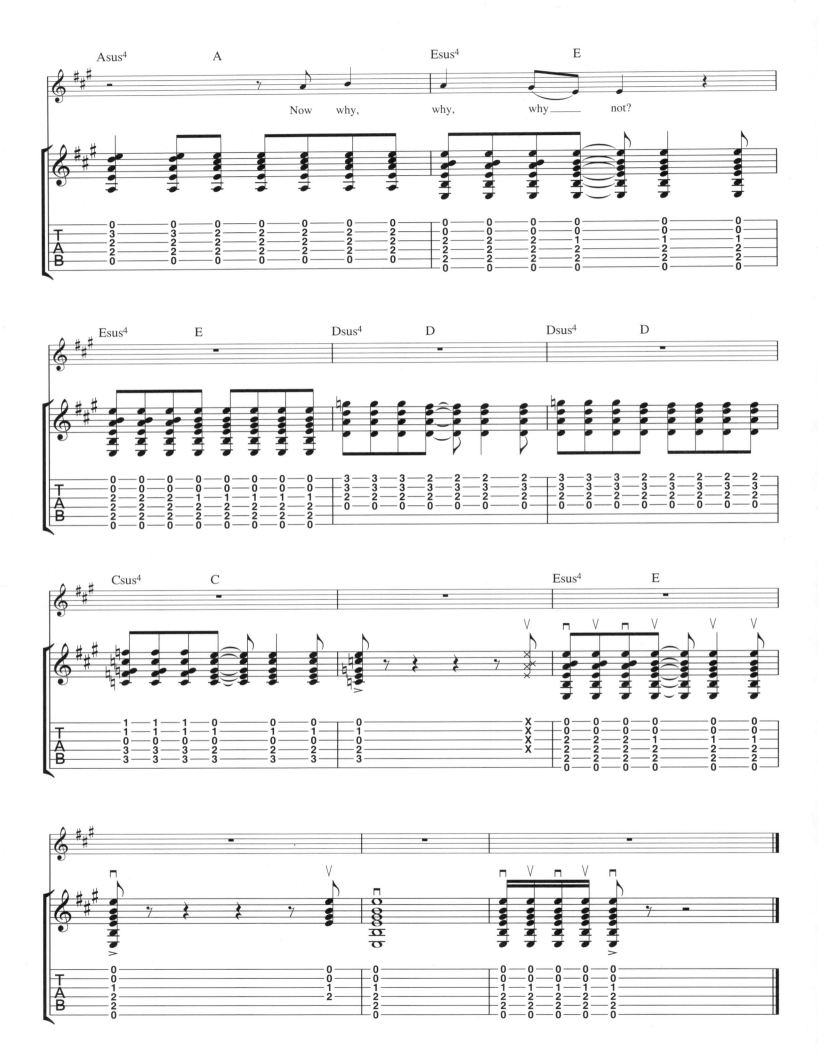

FATHER AND SON

WORDS & MUSIC BY CAT STEVENS

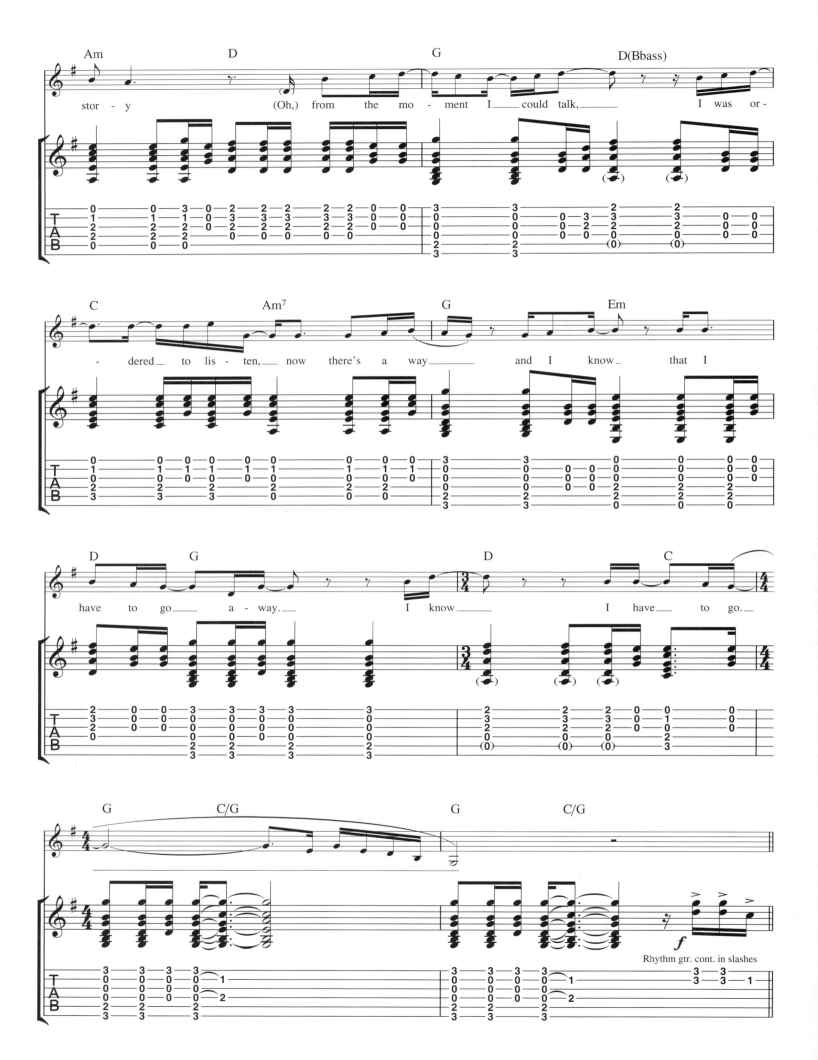

4. It's not time to make a change,___ just sit down___ take it slow - ly. You're still

THE FIRST CUT IS THE DEEPEST

WORDS & MUSIC BY CAT STEVENS

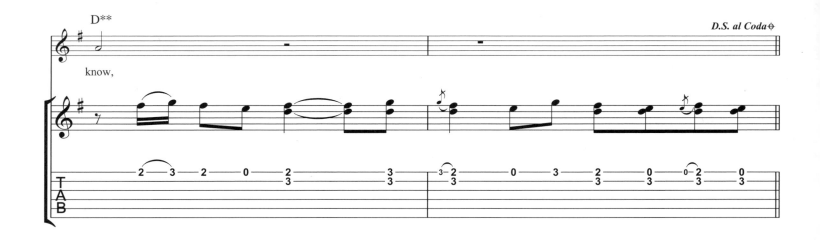

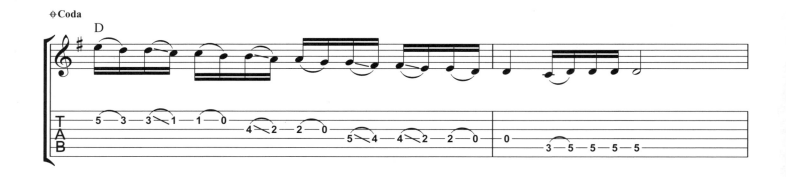

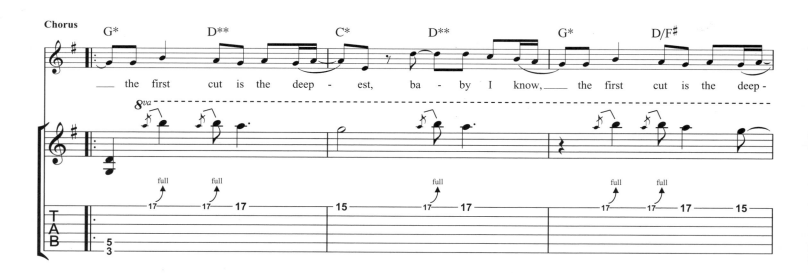

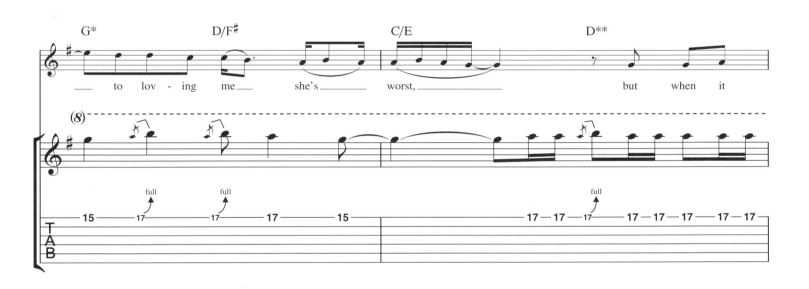

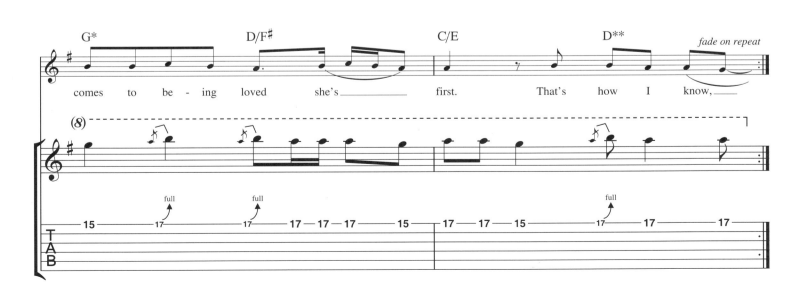

HARD HEADED WOMAN

WORDS & MUSIC BY CAT STEVENS

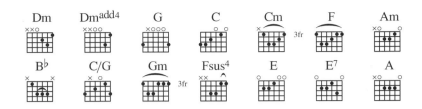

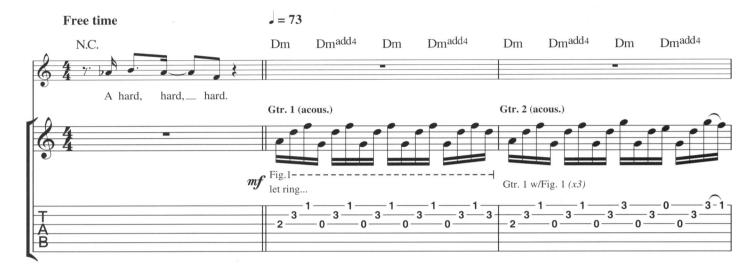

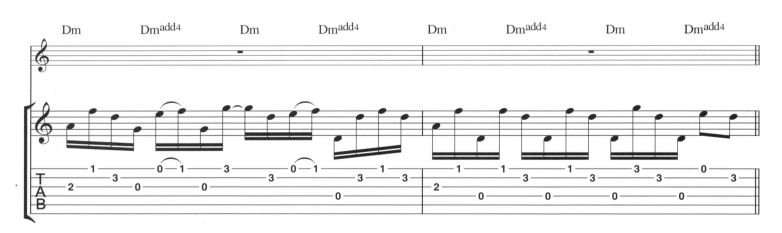

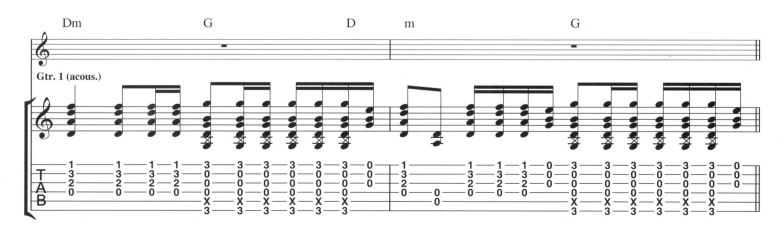

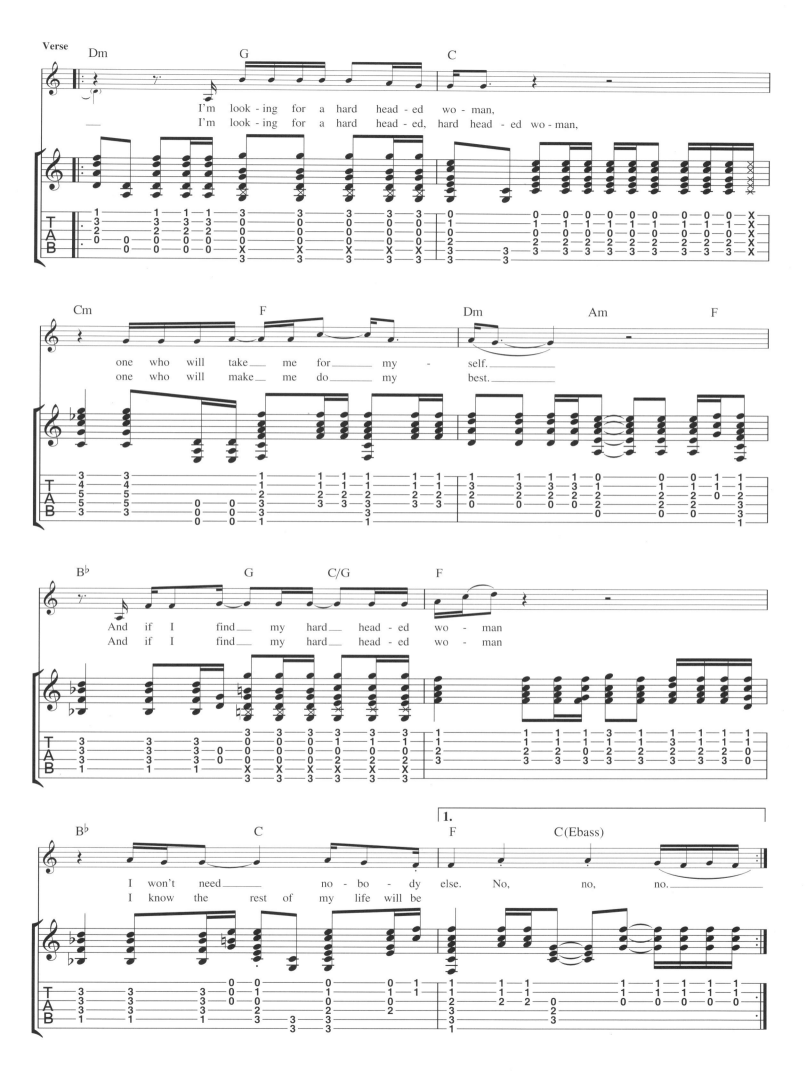

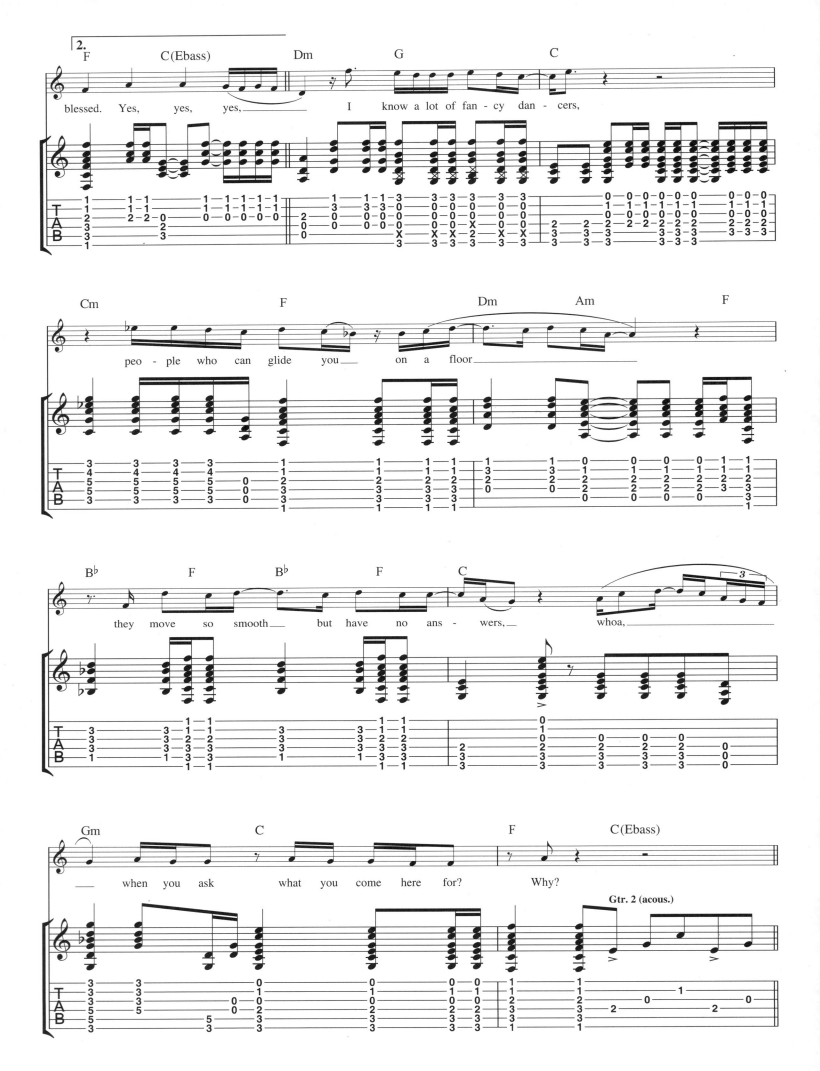

Interlude

Hard head - ed wo - man.

let ring...

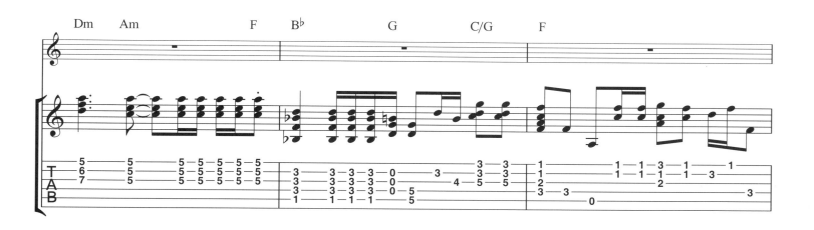

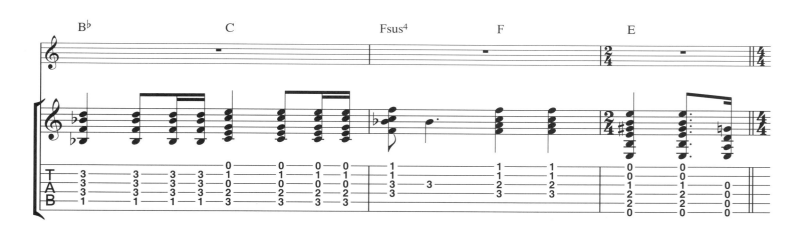

Bridge

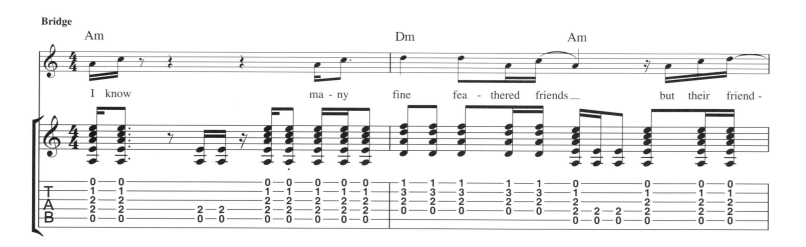

I know   ma - ny   fine   fea - thered   friends___   but their   friend -

43

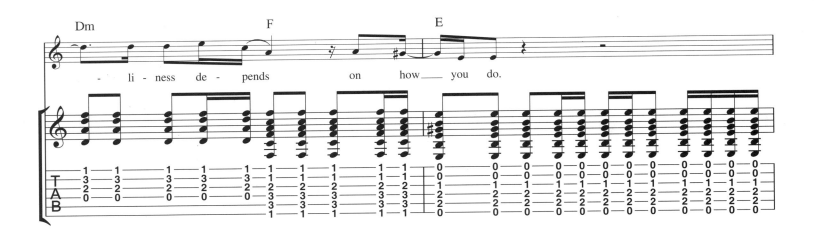

-li - ness de - pends on how___ you do.

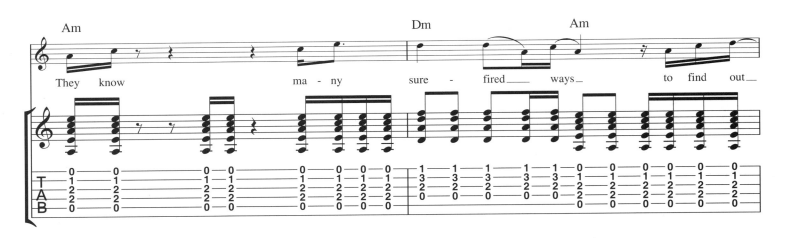

They know ma - ny sure - fired___ ways___ to find out___

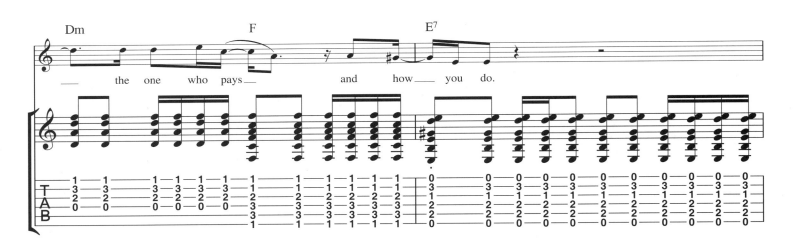

___ the one who pays___ and how___ you do.

Verse

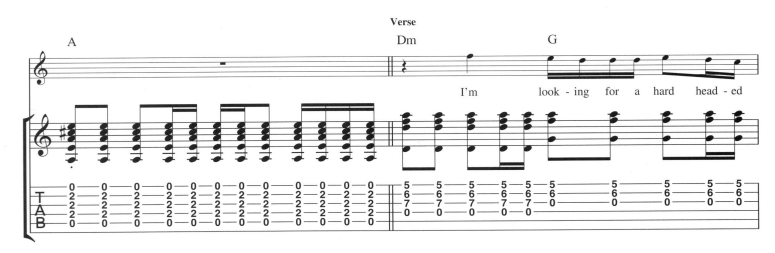

I'm look - ing for a hard head - ed

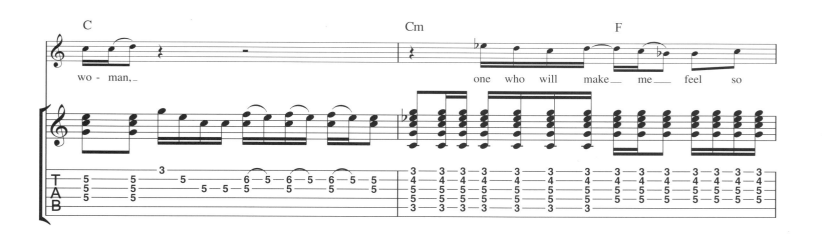

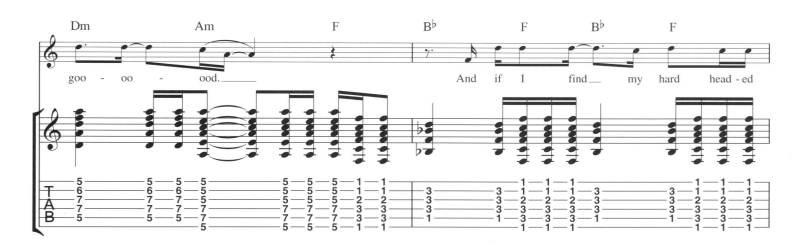

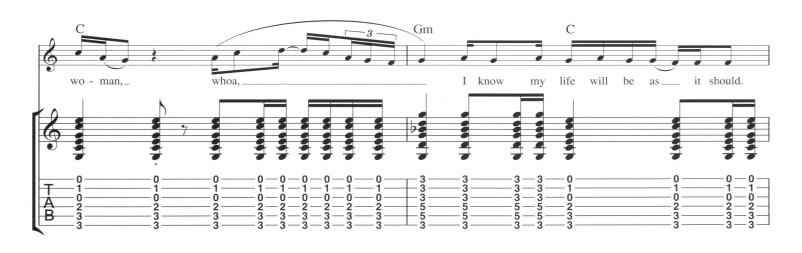

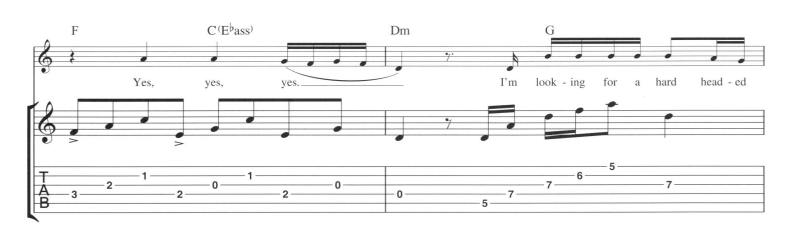

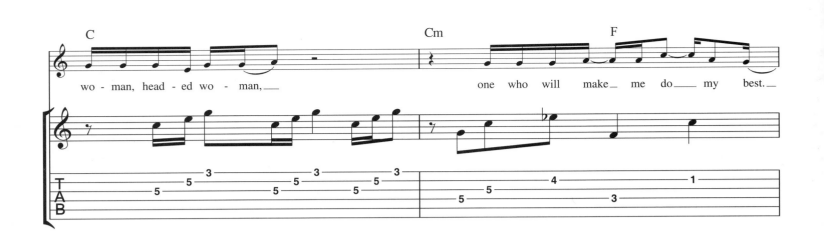

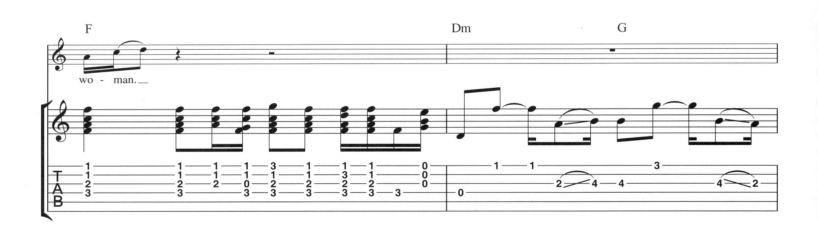

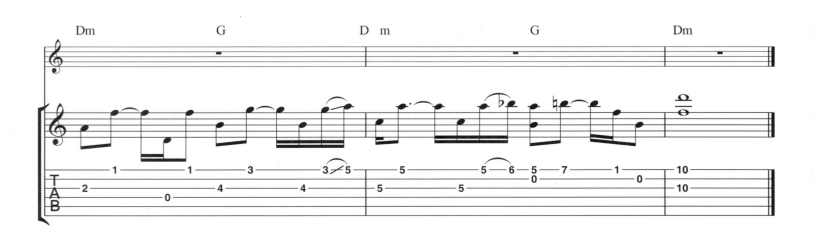

46

HOW CAN I TELL YOU

WORDS & MUSIC BY CAT STEVENS

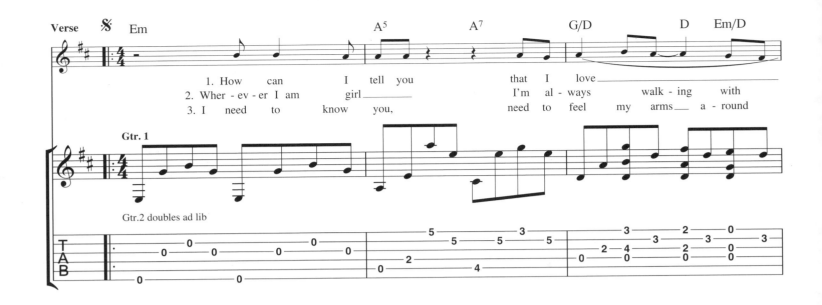

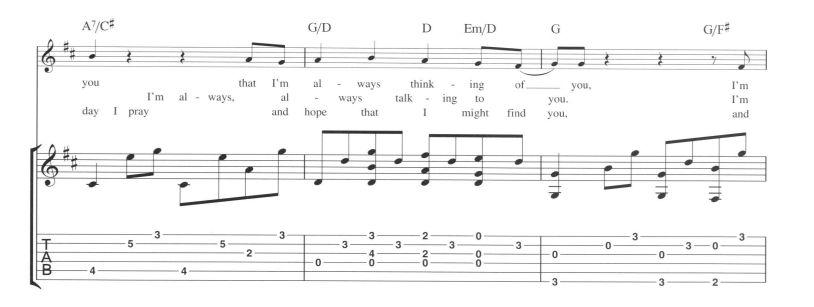

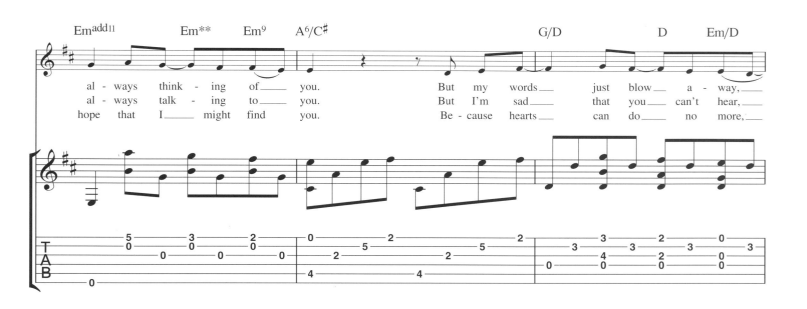

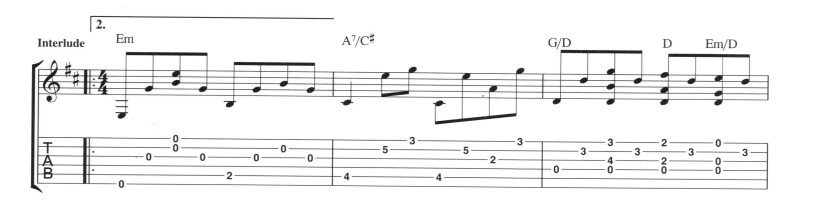

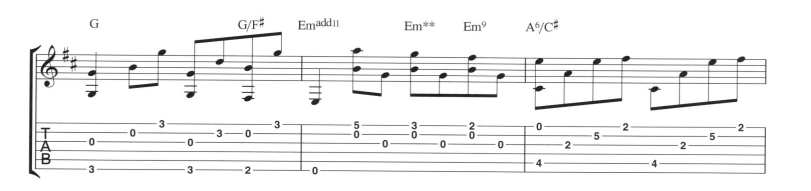

Al - ways ends up to one____ thing ho - ney, still I kneel up - on____ the floor.____

INTO WHITE

WORDS & MUSIC BY CAT STEVENS

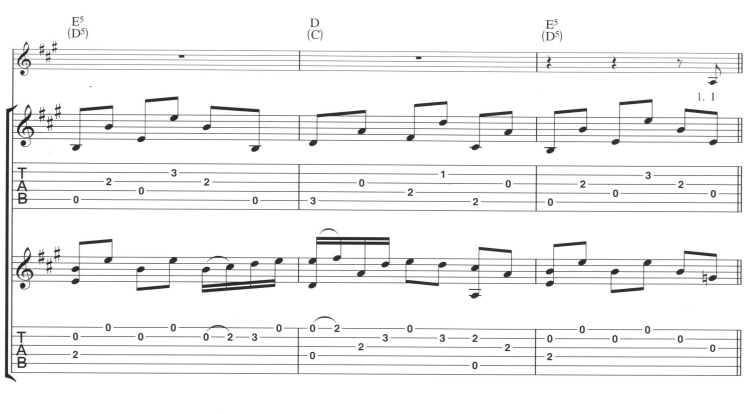

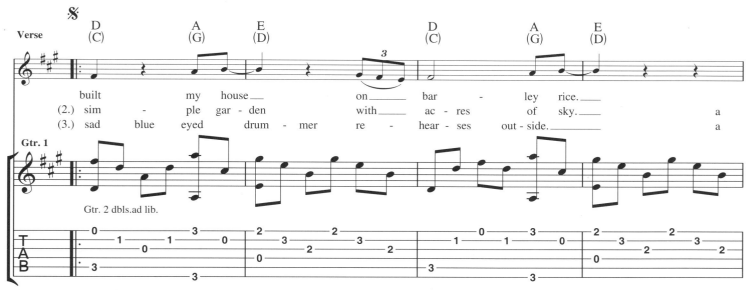

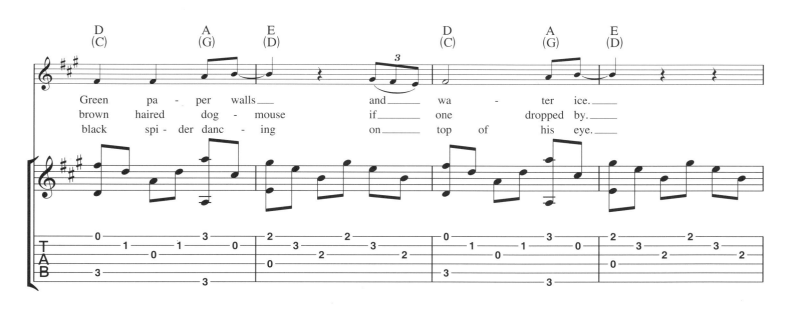

55

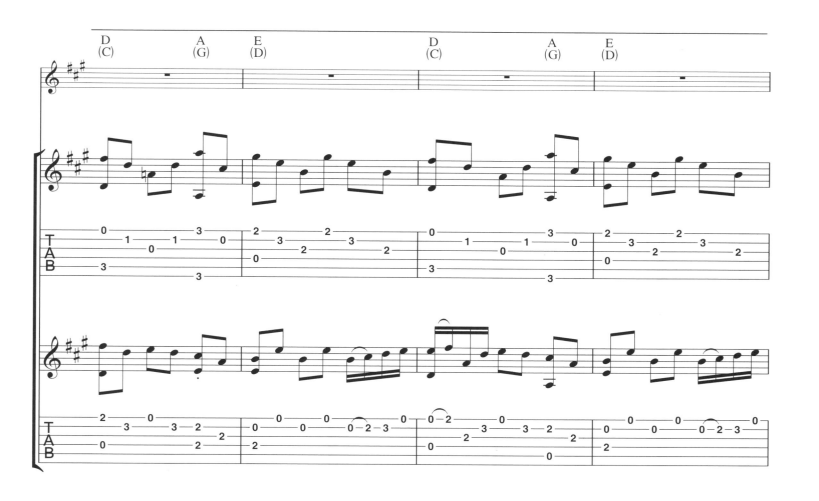

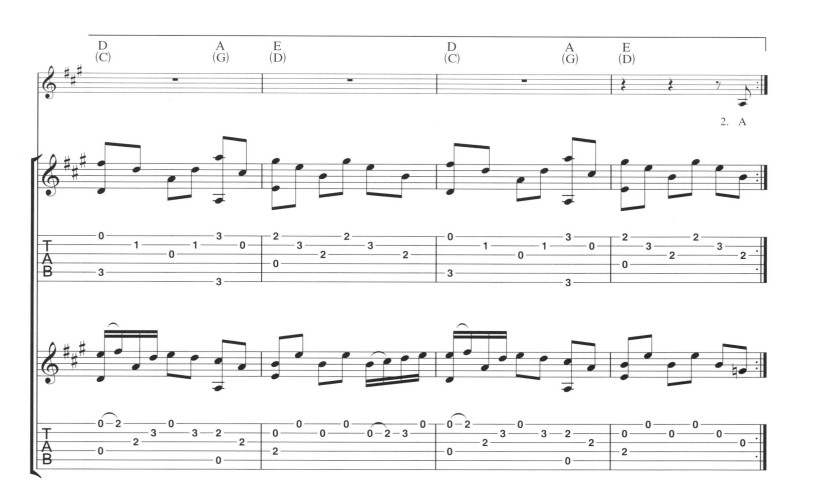

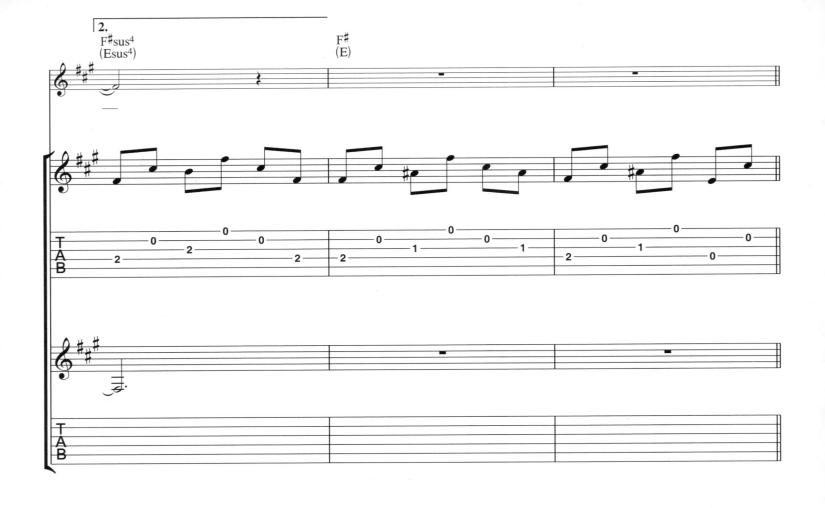

Interlude

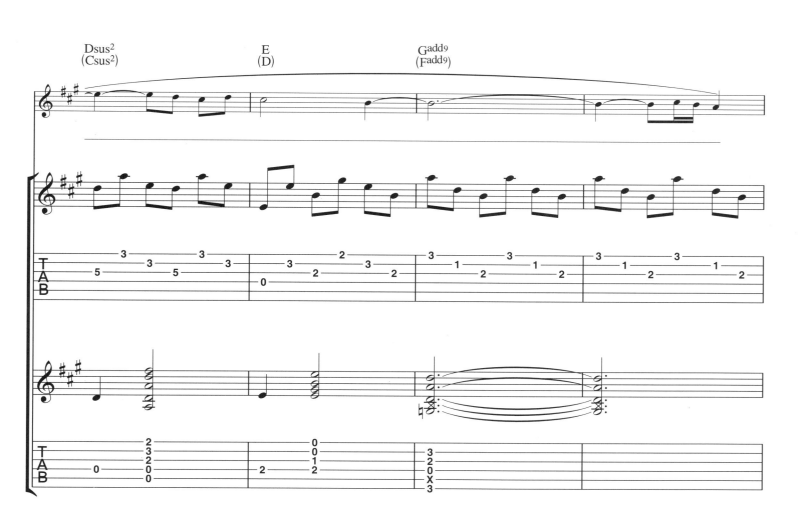

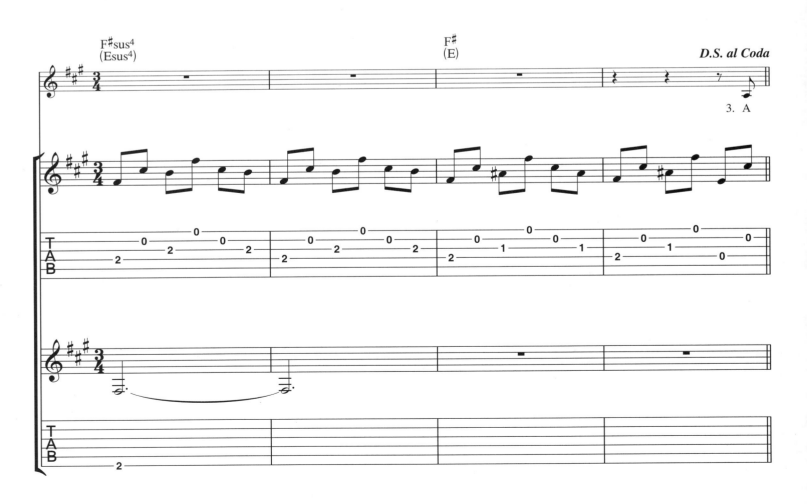

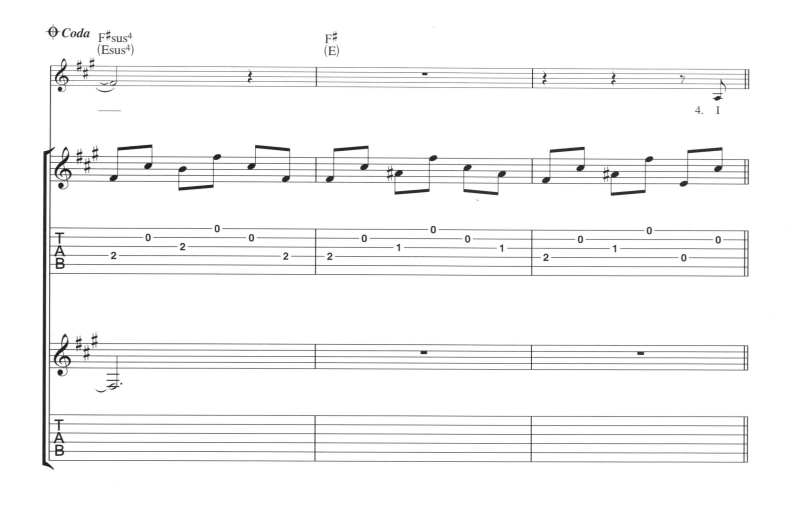

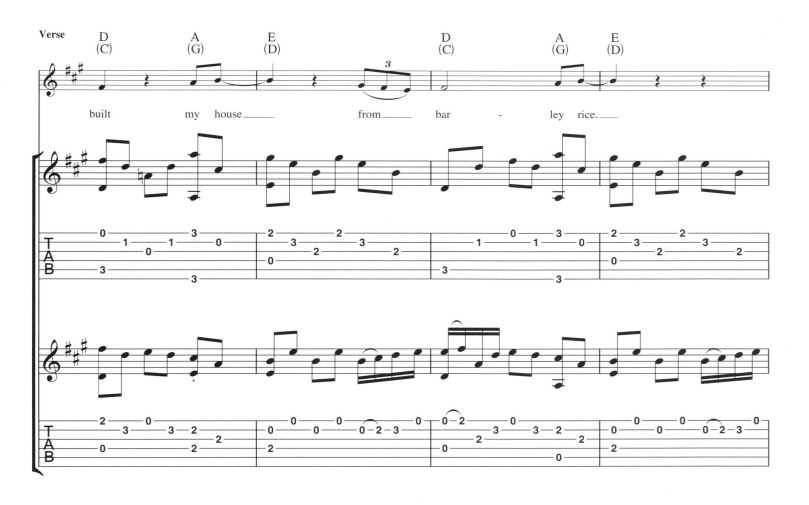

Green pa - per walls____ and____ wa - ter ice.____

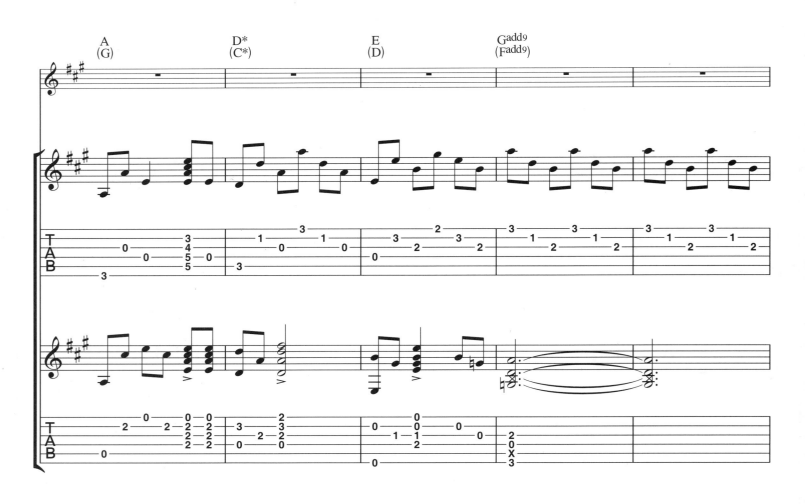

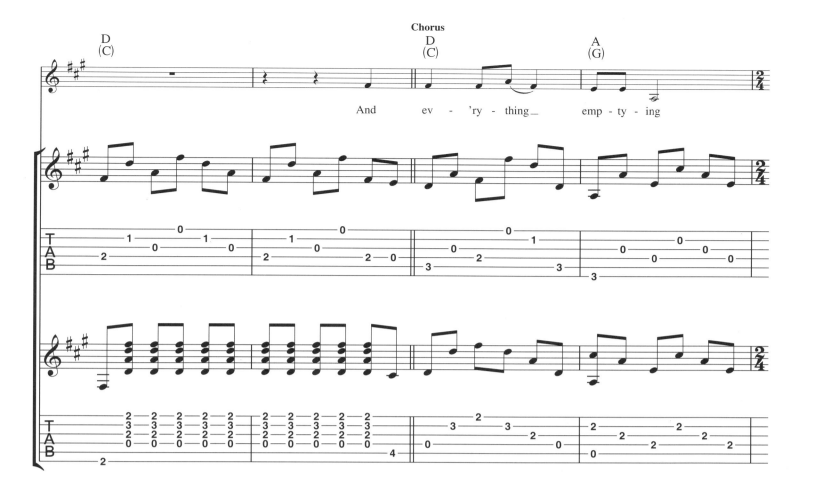

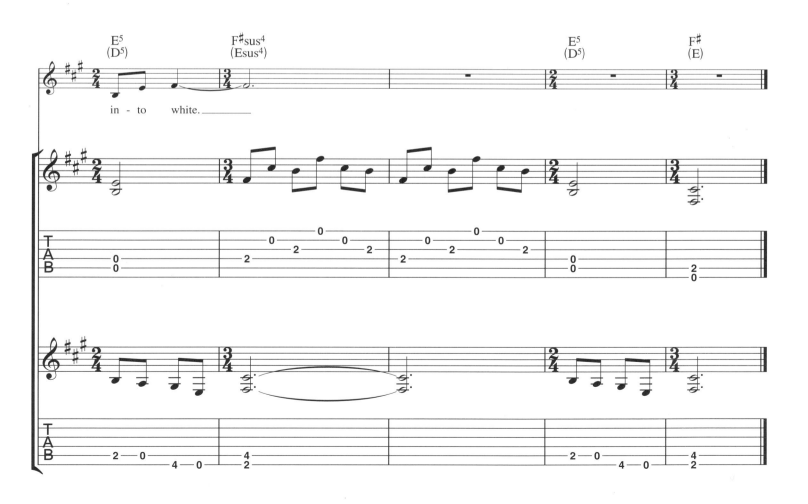

IF I LAUGH

WORDS & MUSIC BY CAT STEVENS

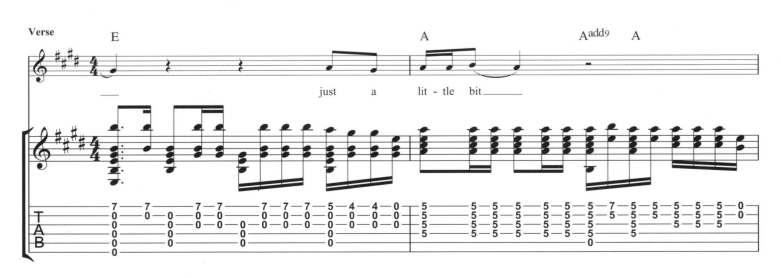

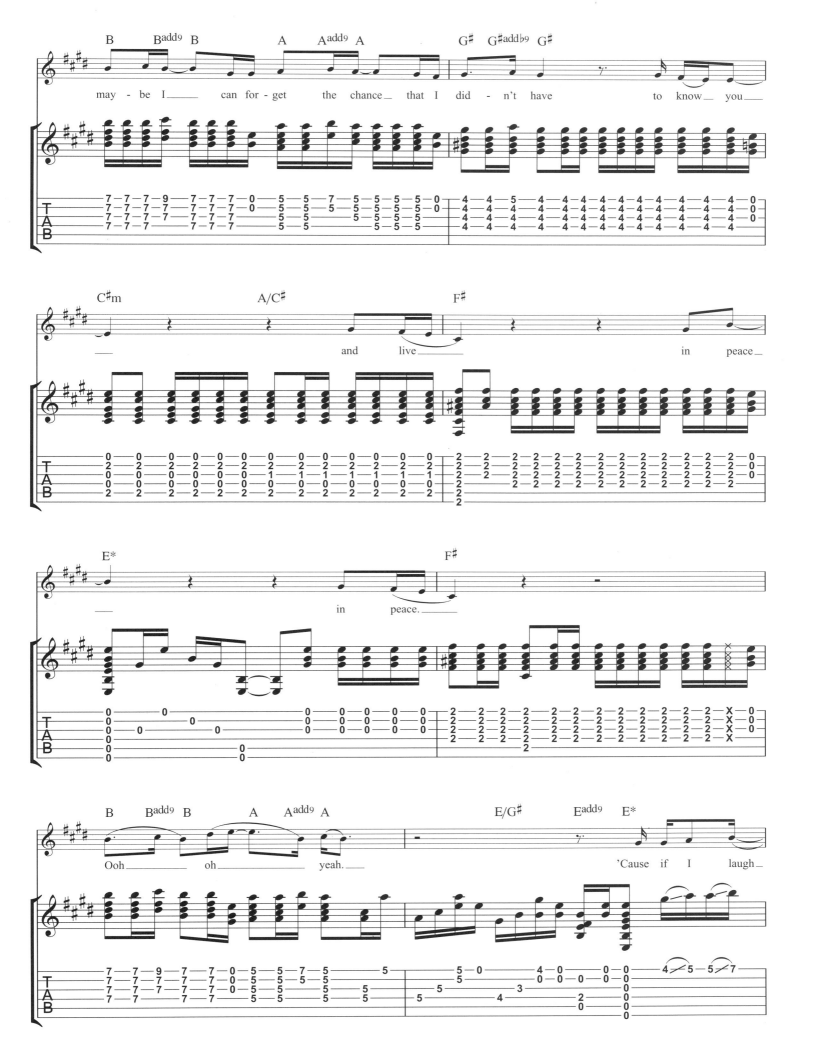

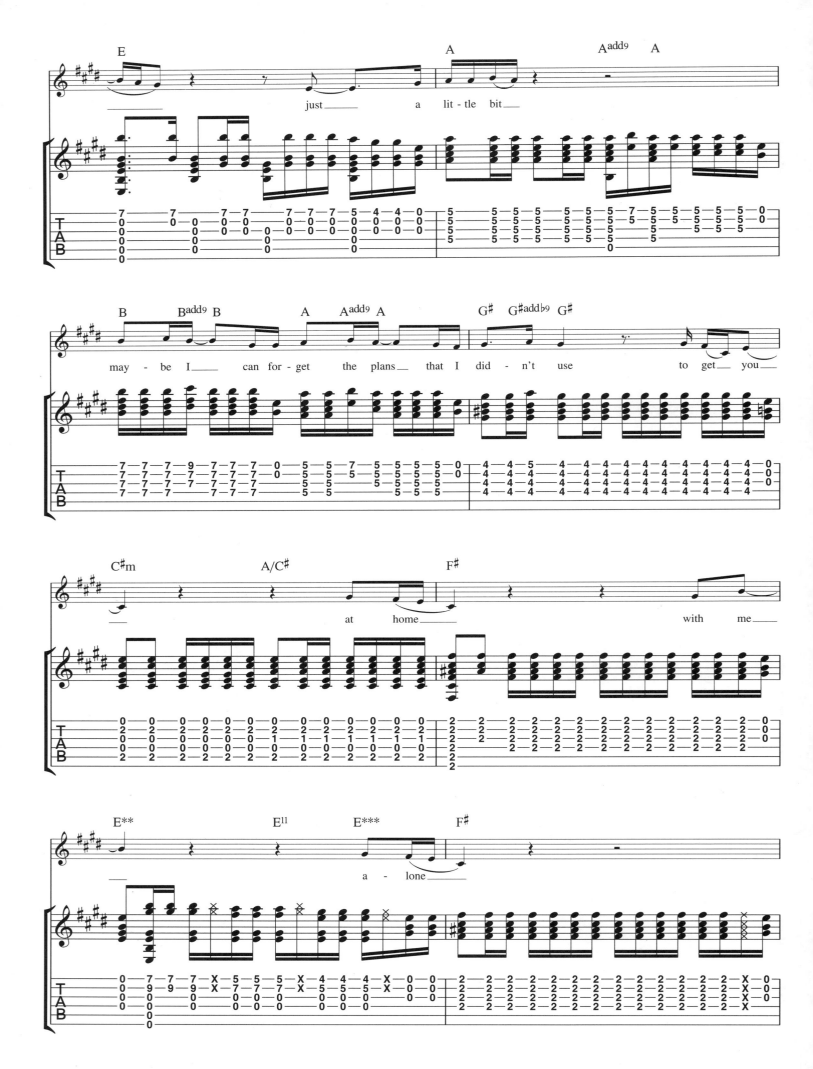

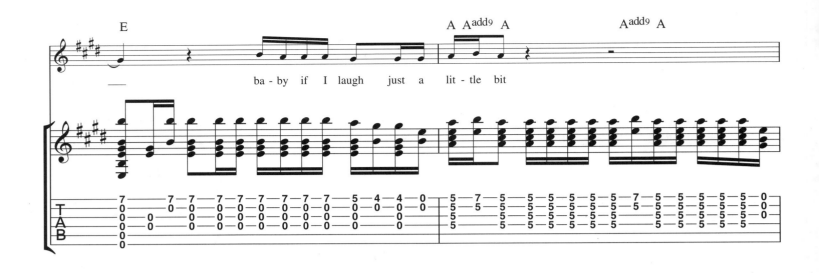

ba - by if I laugh just a lit - tle bit

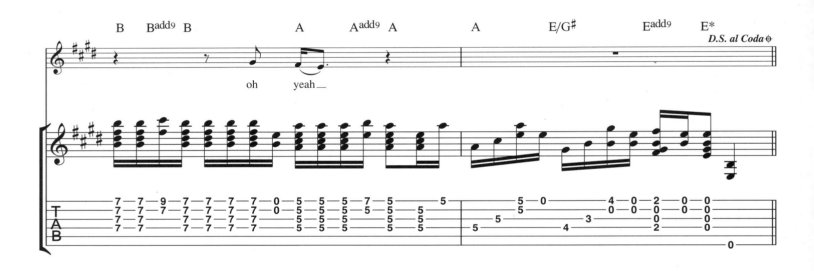

oh yeah —

D.S. al Coda

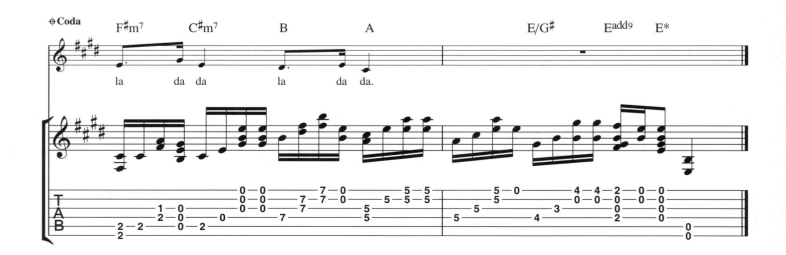

la da da la da da.

Coda

70

LADY D'ARBANVILLE

WORDS & MUSIC BY CAT STEVENS

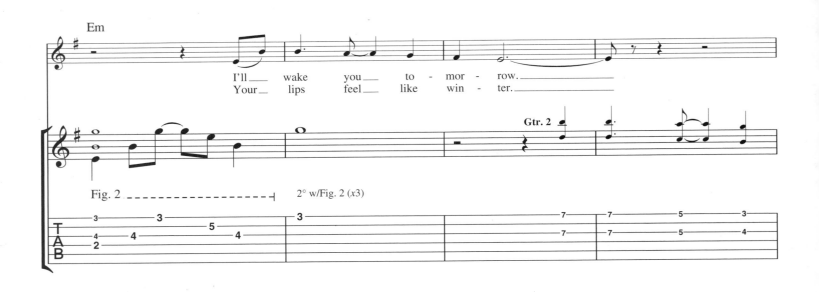

Em

I'll   wake   you   to - mor - row.
Your   lips   feel   like   win - ter.

Gtr. 2

Fig. 2 ‑ ‑ ‑ ‑ ‑ ‑ ‑ ‑ ‑ ‑ ‑ ‑   2° w/Fig. 2 (x3)

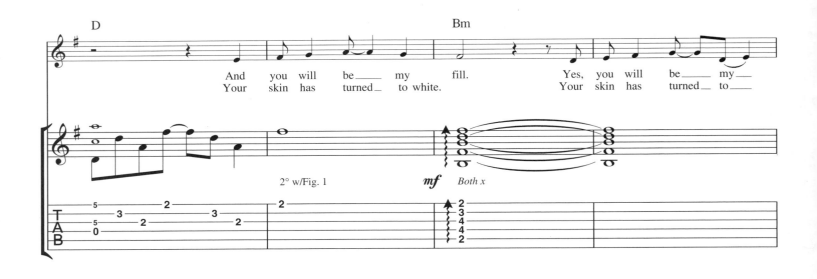

D   Bm

And   you   will   be   my   fill.   Yes,   you   will   be   my
Your   skin   has   turned   to white.   Your   skin   has   turned   to

2° w/Fig. 1   *mf*   *Both x*

% Verse

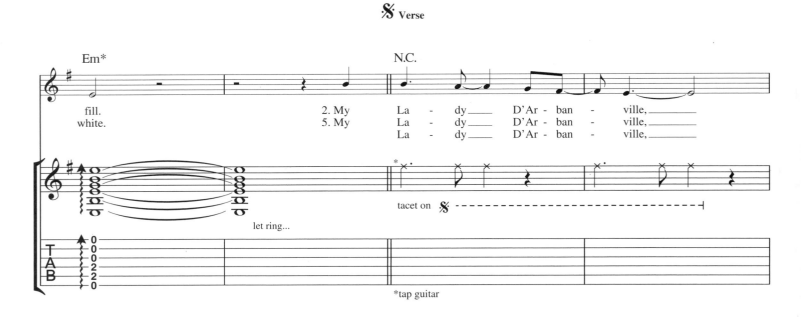

Em*   N.C.

fill.   2. My   La - dy   D'Ar - ban - ville,
white.   5. My   La - dy   D'Ar - ban - ville,
                             La - dy   D'Ar - ban - ville,

let ring...

tacet on % ‑ ‑ ‑ ‑ ‑ ‑ ‑ ‑ ‑ ‑ ‑ ‑ ‑ ‑ ‑ ‑ ‑ ‑ ‑

*tap guitar

72

why does it grieve___ me___ so?
why do you sleep___ so___ still?
why do you grieve___ me___ so?

But your___ heart seems so sil - ent.
I'll___ wake you___ to - mor - row.
But your___ heart seems so sil - ent.

Why do you breathe___ so low,___ why
And you will be___ my fill,___ yes
Why do you breathe___ so low, why

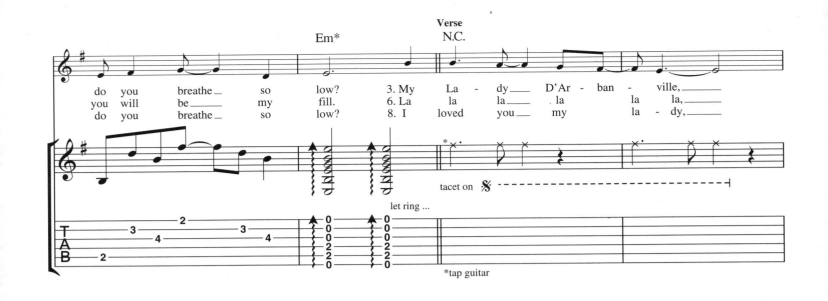

MOONSHADOW

WORDS & MUSIC BY CAT STEVENS

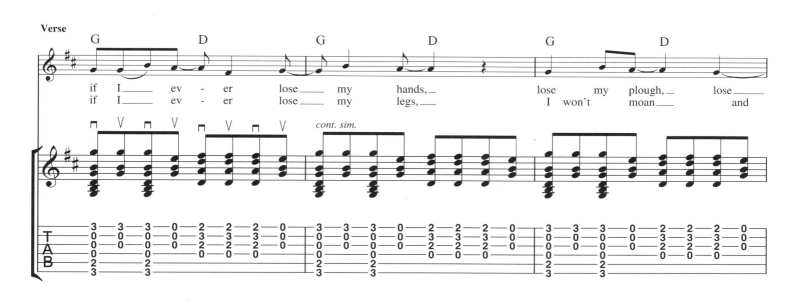

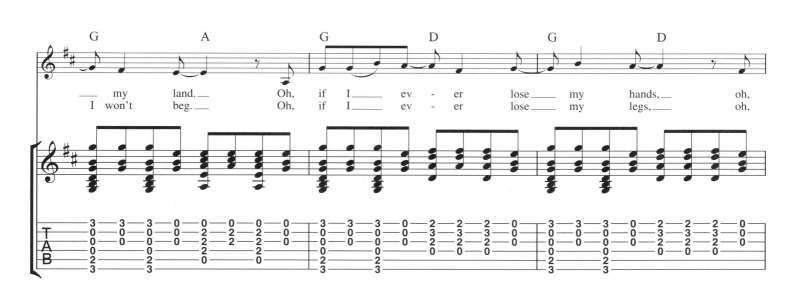

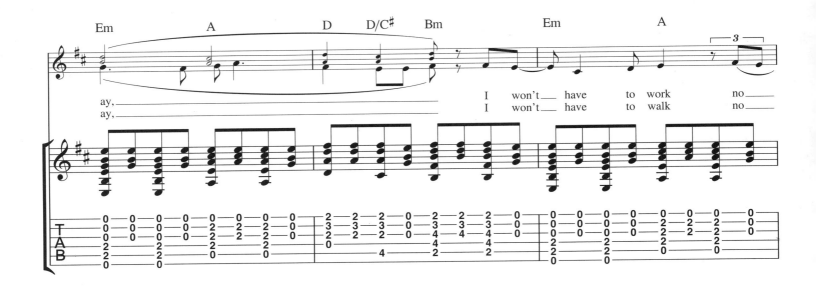

ay, _____
ay, _____
I won't___ have to work no_____
I won't___ have to walk no_____

___ more.
___ more.
And if I___ ev – er lose___ my eyes,___
And if I___ ev – er lose___ my mouth,___

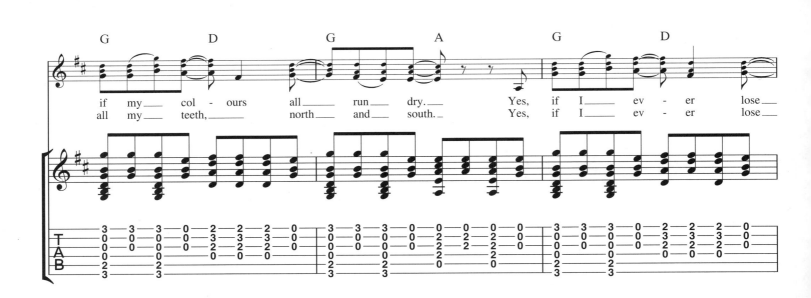

if my___ col - ours all___ run___ dry.
all my___ teeth, north and___ south.
Yes, if I___ ev – er lose___
Yes, if I___ ev – er lose___

Middle 8

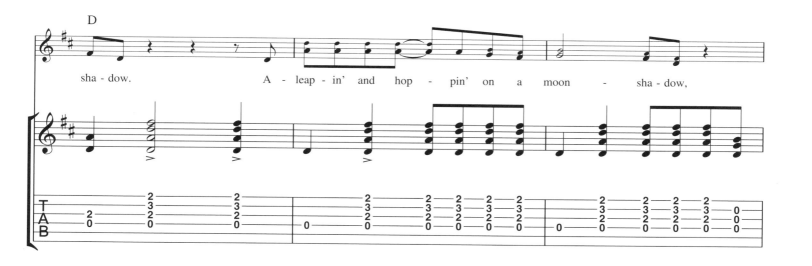

sha - dow.   A - leap - in' and hop - pin' on a moon - sha - dow,

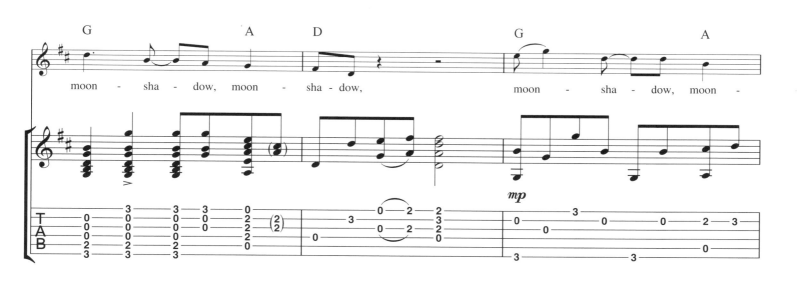

moon - sha - dow, moon - sha - dow,   moon - sha - dow, moon -

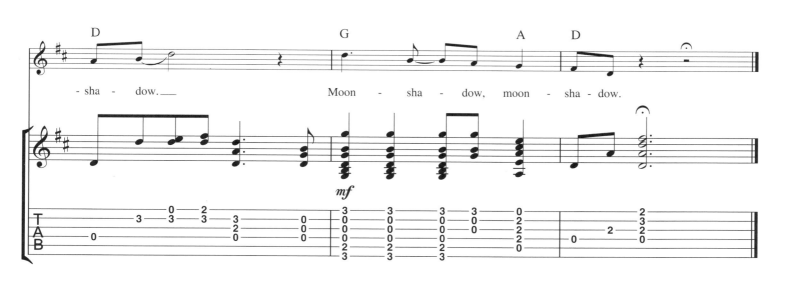

- sha - dow.___   Moon - sha - dow, moon - sha - dow.

OH VERY YOUNG

WORDS & MUSIC BY CAT STEVENS

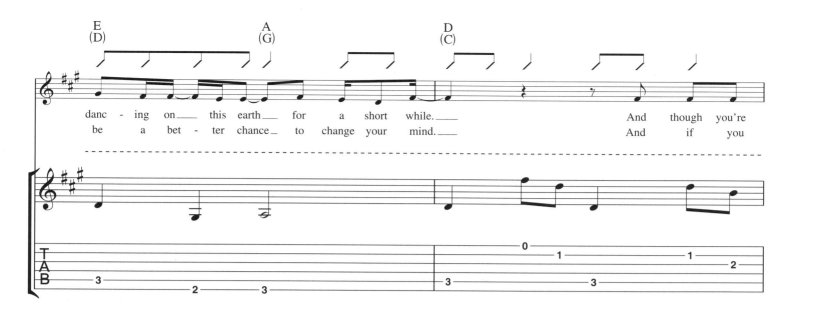

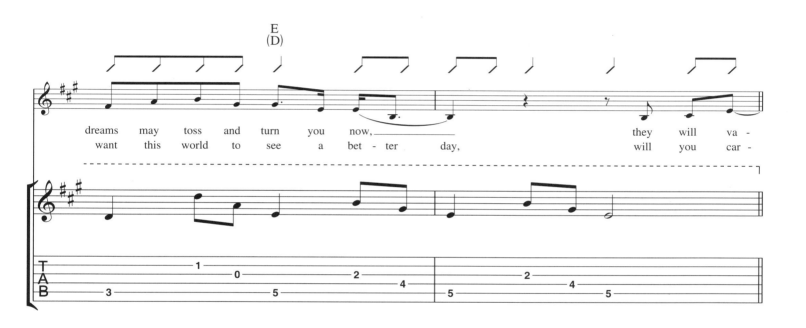

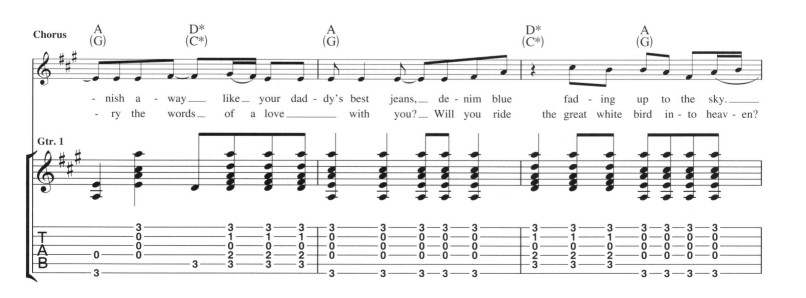

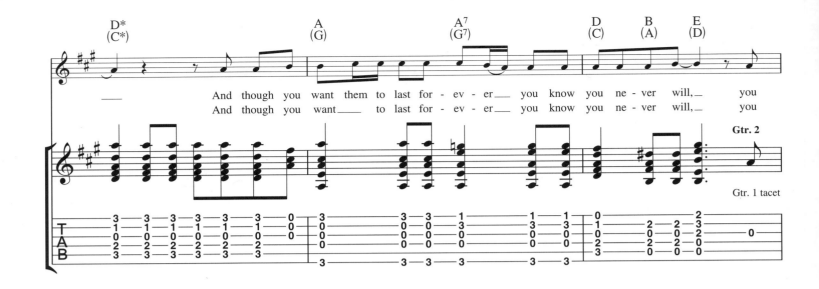

And though you want them to last for - ev - er__ you know you ne - ver will,__ you
And though you want__ to last for - ev - er__ you know you ne - ver will,__ you

know you ne - ver will,____ and the patch - es make__ the good - bye hard - er
know you ne - ver will,____ and the good - bye makes__ the jour - ney hard - er

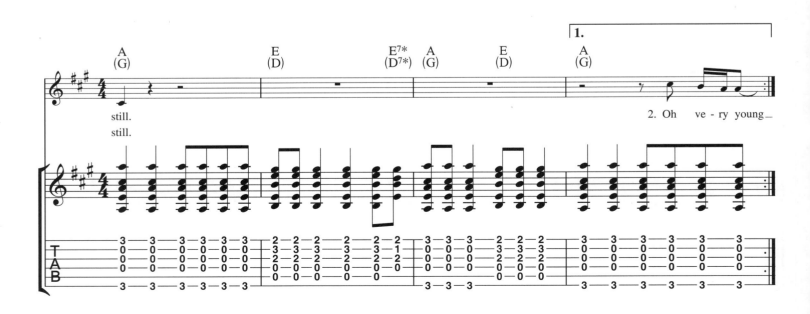

still.
still.

2. Oh ve - ry young__

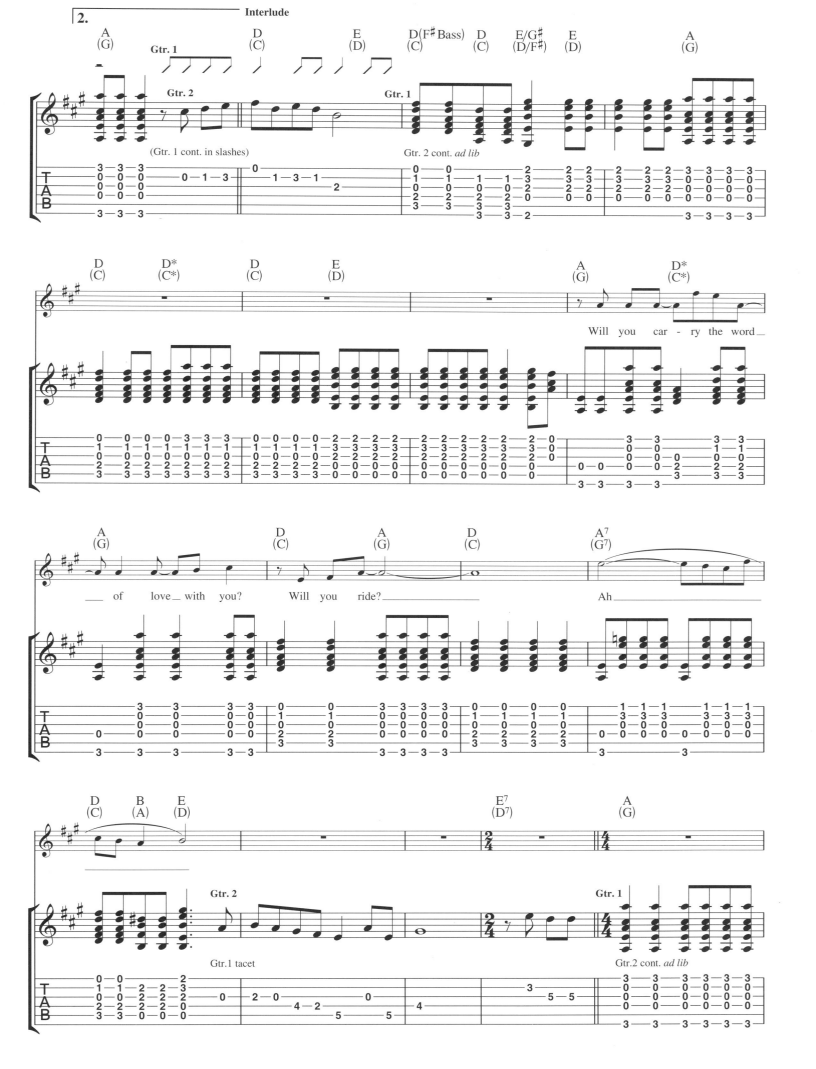

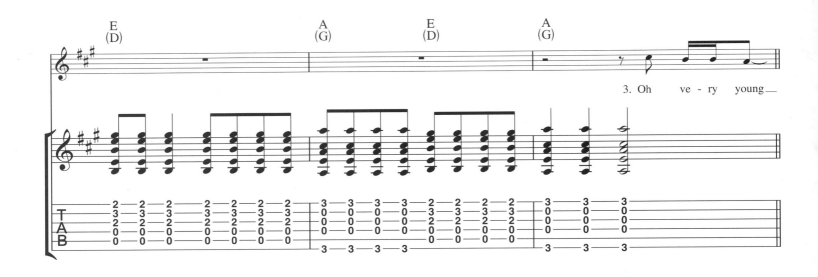

3. Oh ve - ry young

Verse

— what will you leave— us this time?—   You're on - ly danc - ing on— this earth   for a short while.—

Gtr. 2

Gtr. 2 tacet

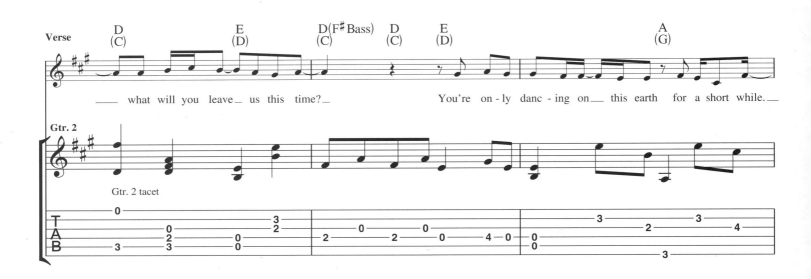

rall.

— Oh— ve - ry young what will you   leave— us   this time?

Gtrs. 1+2

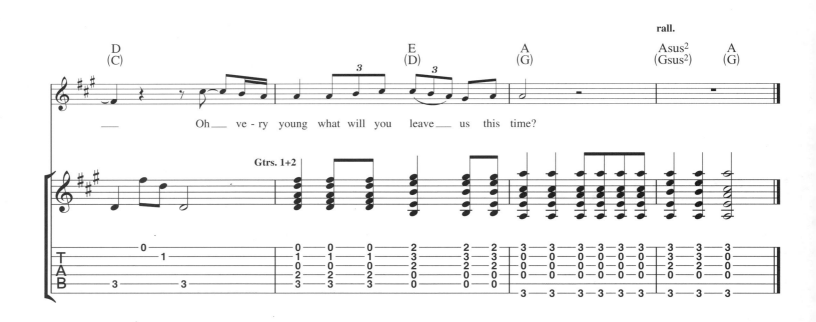

PEACE TRAIN

WORDS & MUSIC BY CAT STEVENS

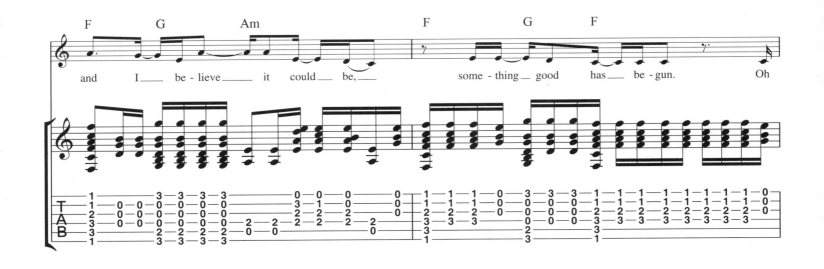

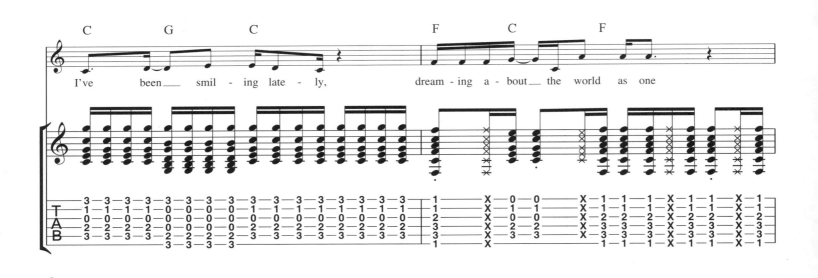

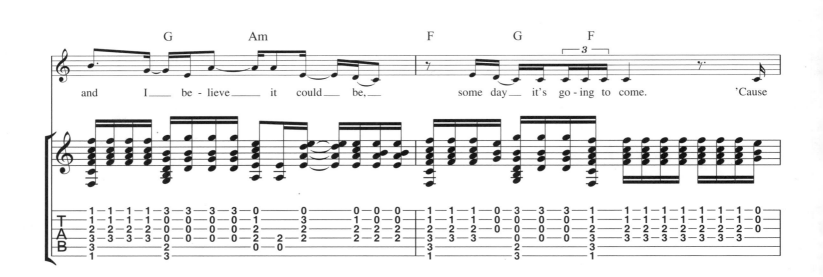

Verse

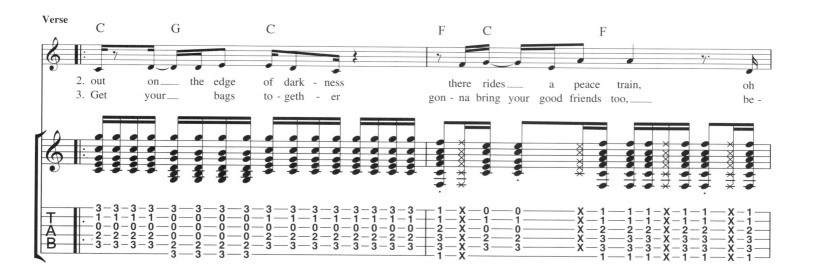

2. out on the edge of dark-ness there rides a peace train, oh
3. Get your bags to-geth-er gon-na bring your good friends too, be-

peace train take this coun-try, come take me home a-gain. Now
-cause it's get-ting near-er, it soon will be with you. And

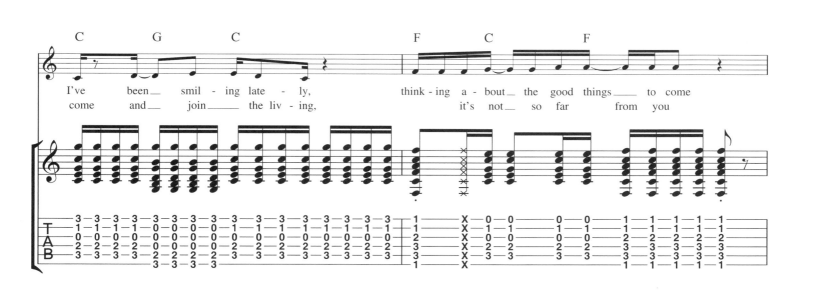

I've been smil-ing late - ly, think-ing a-bout the good things to come
come and join the liv-ing, it's not so far from you

Chorus 𝄋

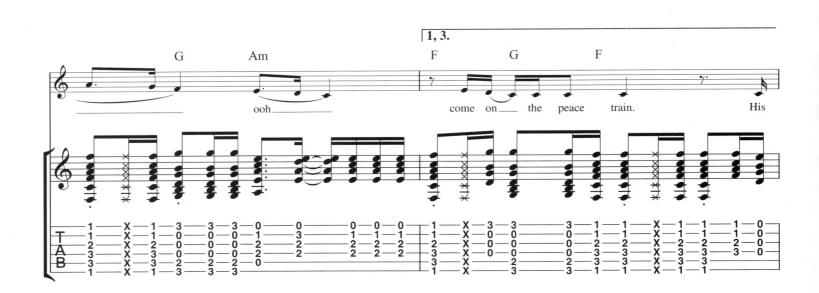

peace train,___ ho - ly roll - er, ev - ery - one get up on the peace train.

Ooh_____ ooh_____ come on___ the peace train.

2.

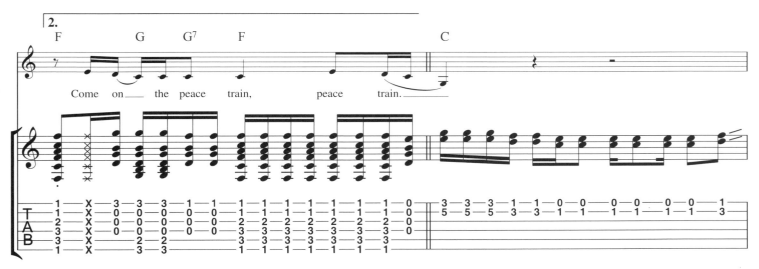

Come on___ the peace train, peace train.___

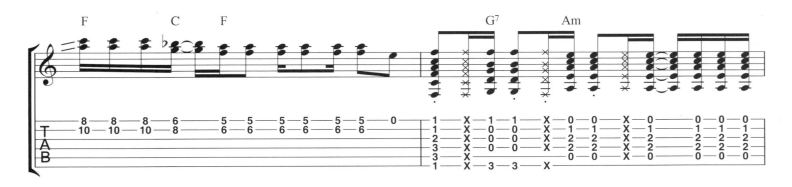

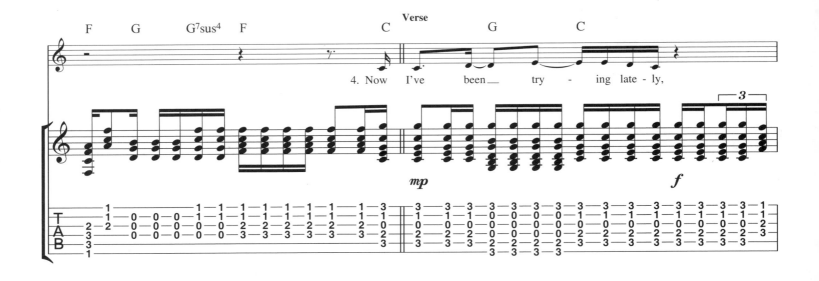

4. Now I've been__ try - ing late - ly,

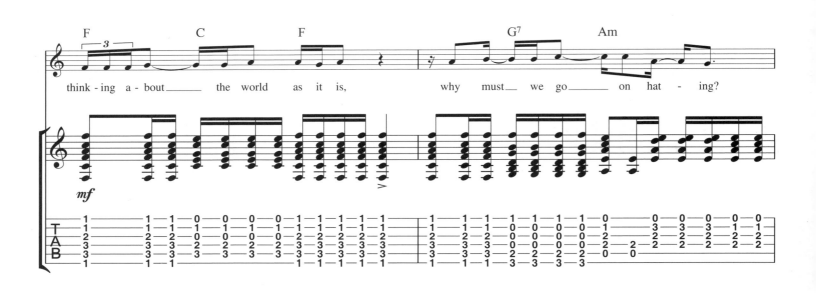

think - ing a - bout__ the world as it is, why must__ we go__ on hat - ing?

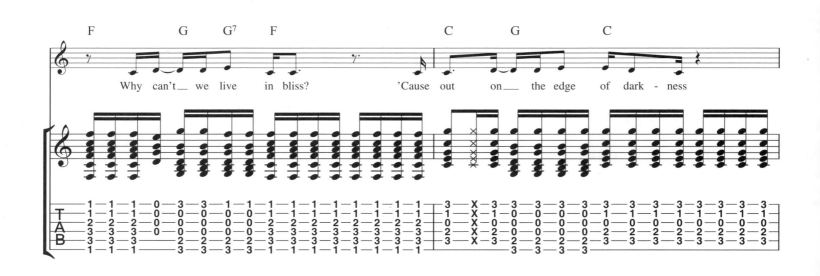

Why can't__ we live in bliss? 'Cause out on__ the edge of dark - ness

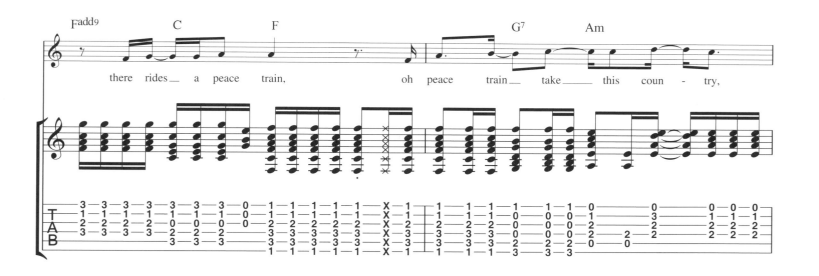

there rides a peace train, oh peace train take this coun - try,

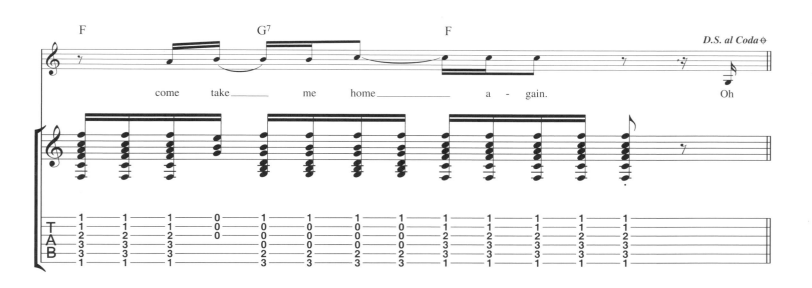

come take me home a - gain. Oh

D.S. al Coda ✛

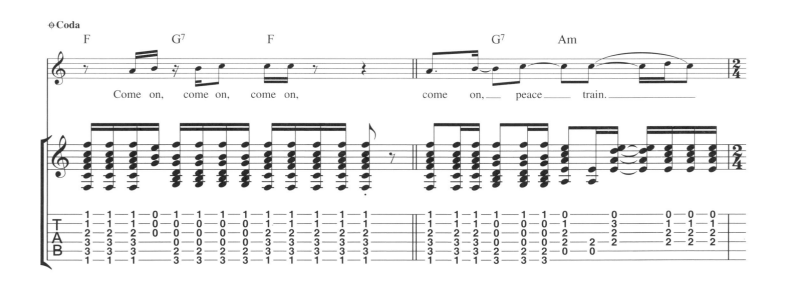

✛ **Coda**

Come on, come on, come on, come on, peace train.

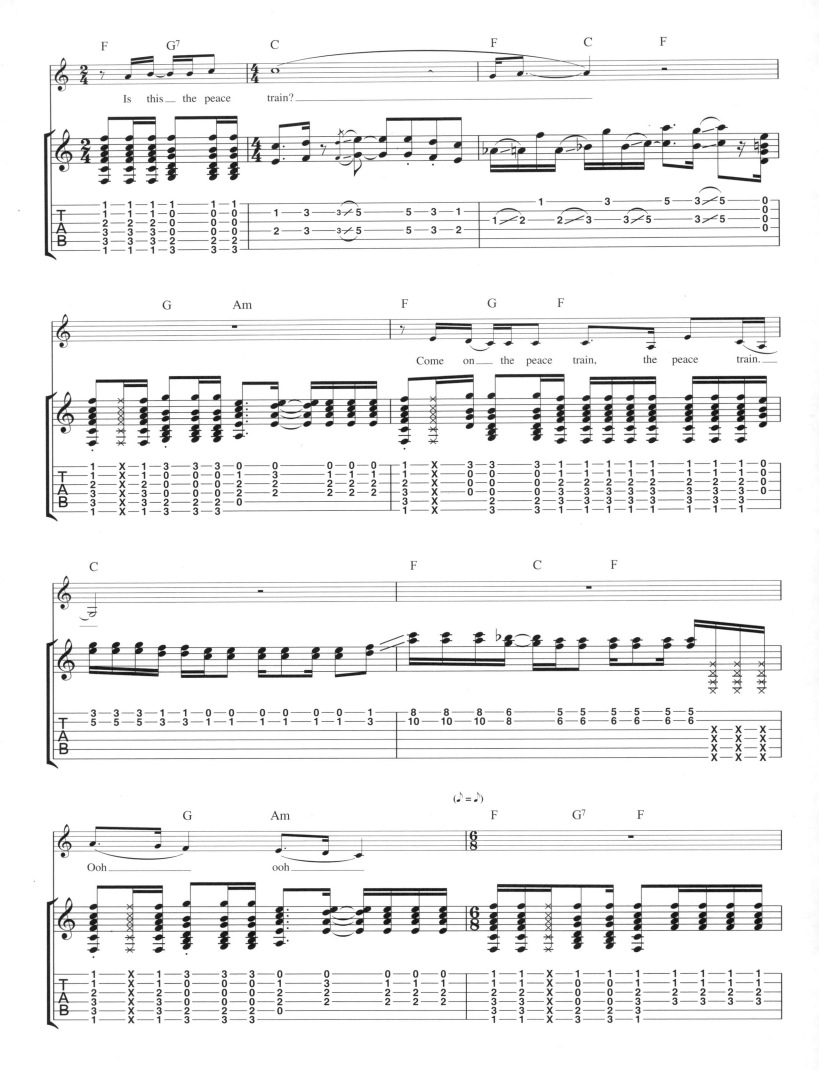

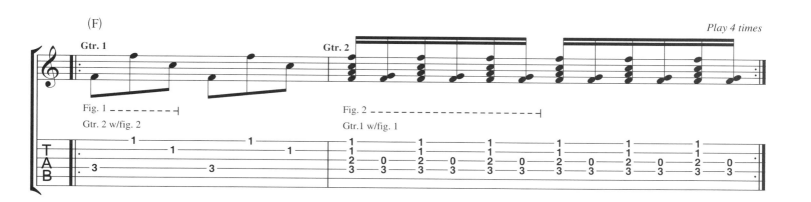
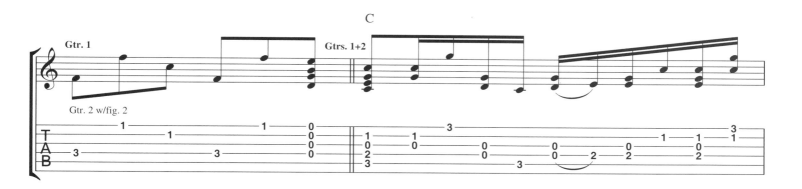
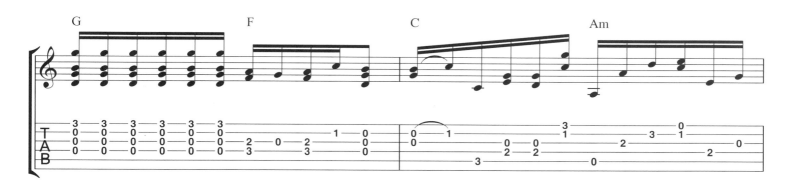
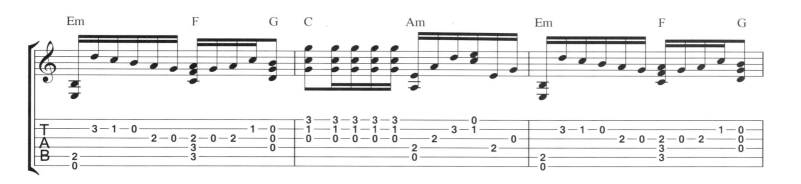
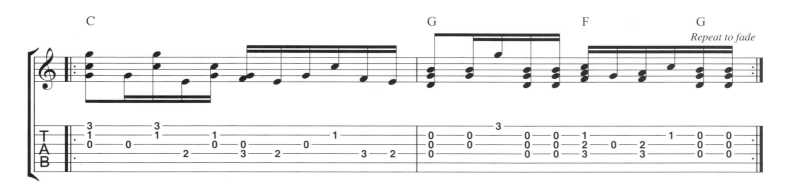

SUN / C79

WORDS & MUSIC BY CAT STEVENS

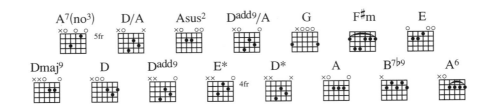

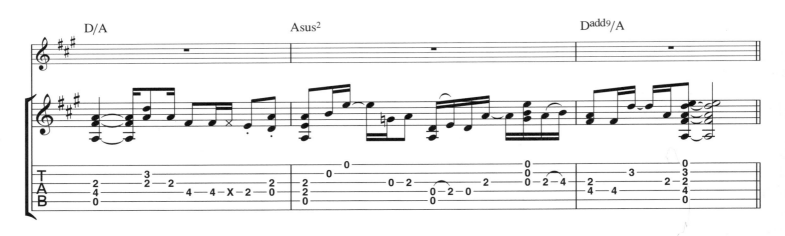

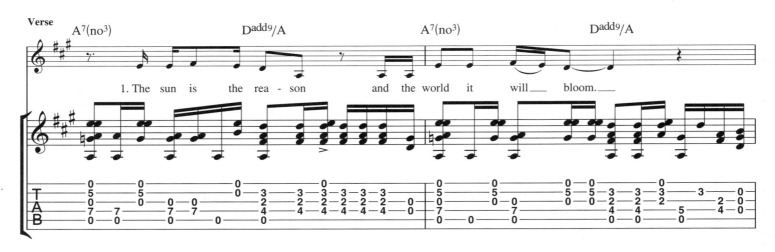

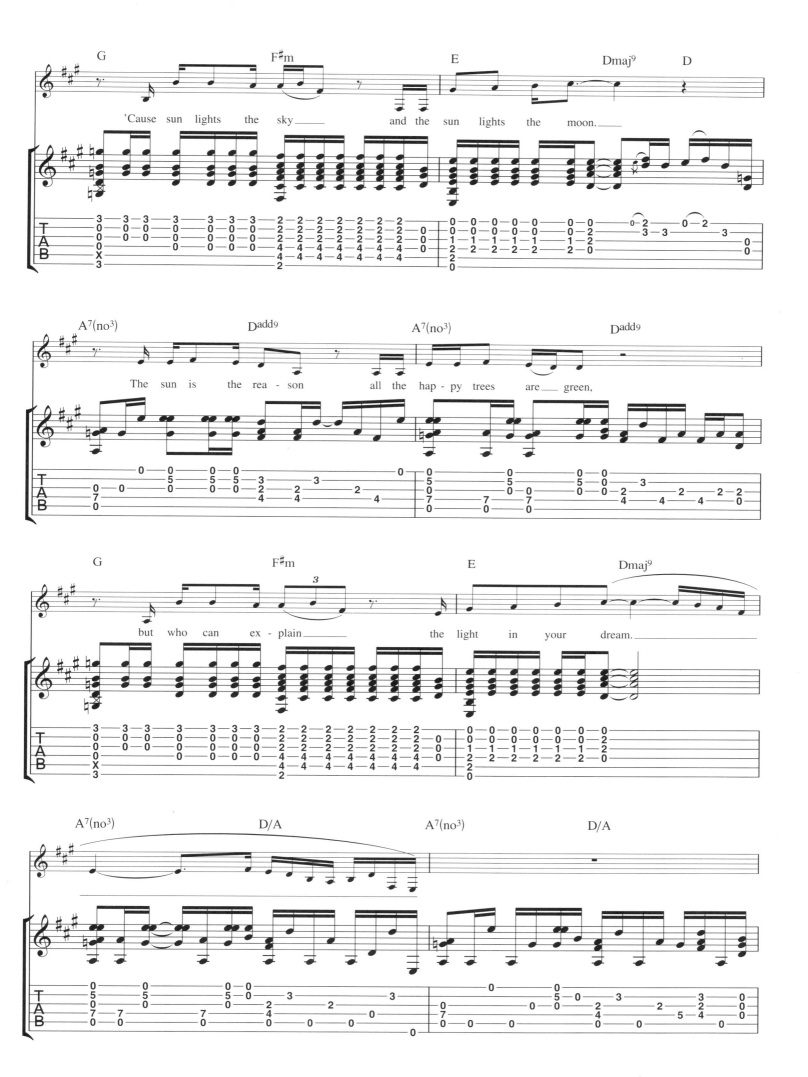

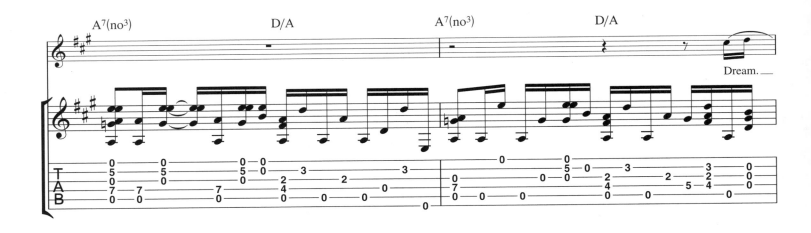

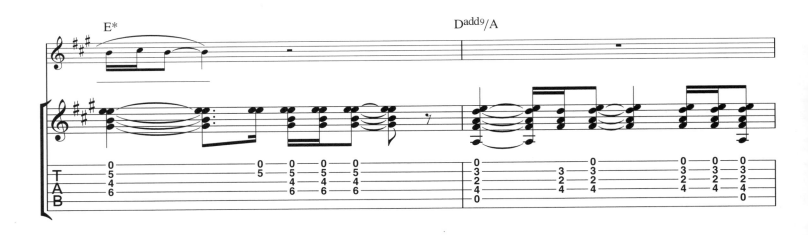

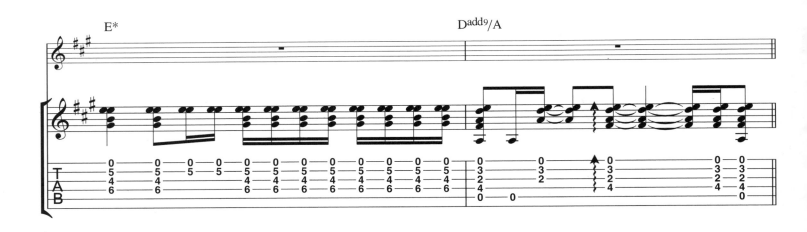

2. Sit you down,___ sit you down___ young gen - tle - men,___
3. We met in the back row_____ be - hind the stage,___

there's some-thing I want you to know.
she had the best fi-gure by far. oh.

You keep on ask-ing me, you keep on ask-ing me why, why are we here,
A thou-sand hours I looked at her eyes,

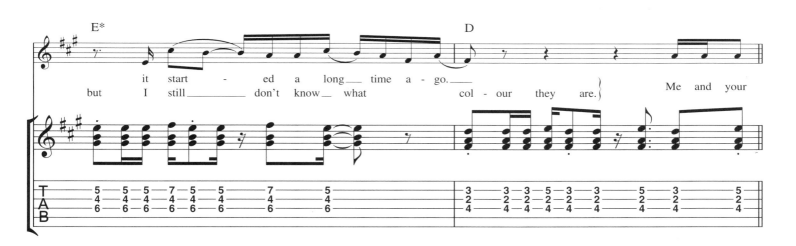

it start-ed a long time a-go.
but I still don't know what col-our they are. Me and your

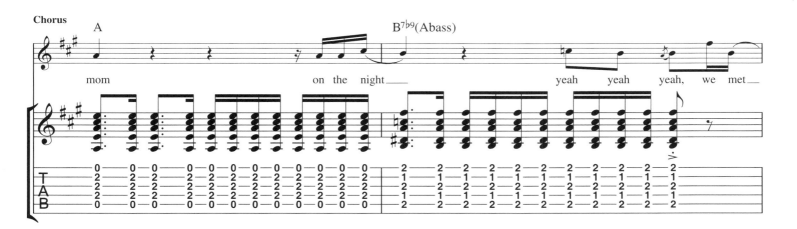

Chorus

mom on the night yeah yeah yeah, we met

101

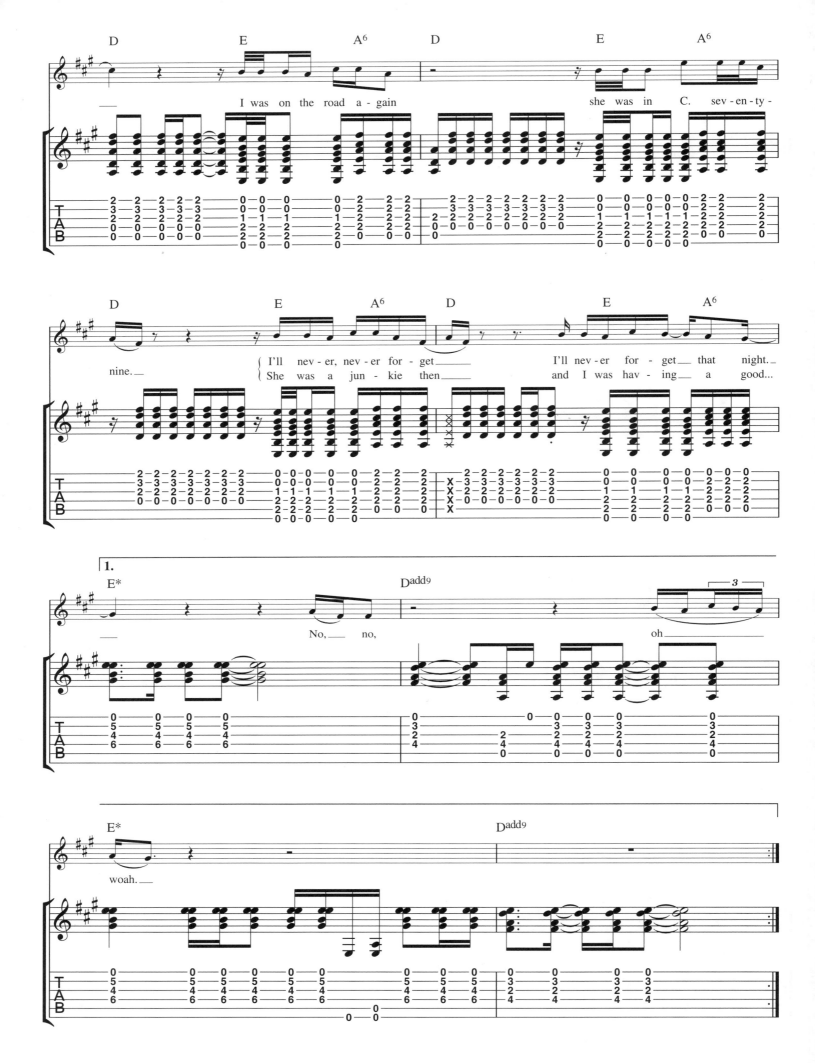

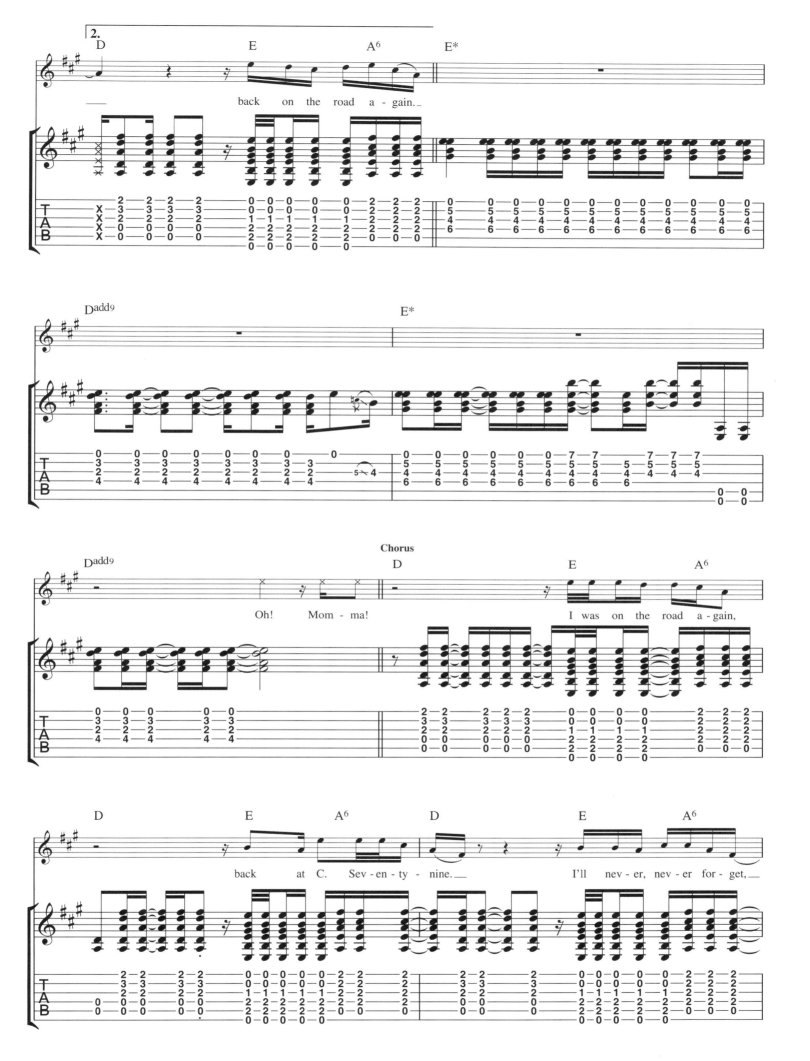

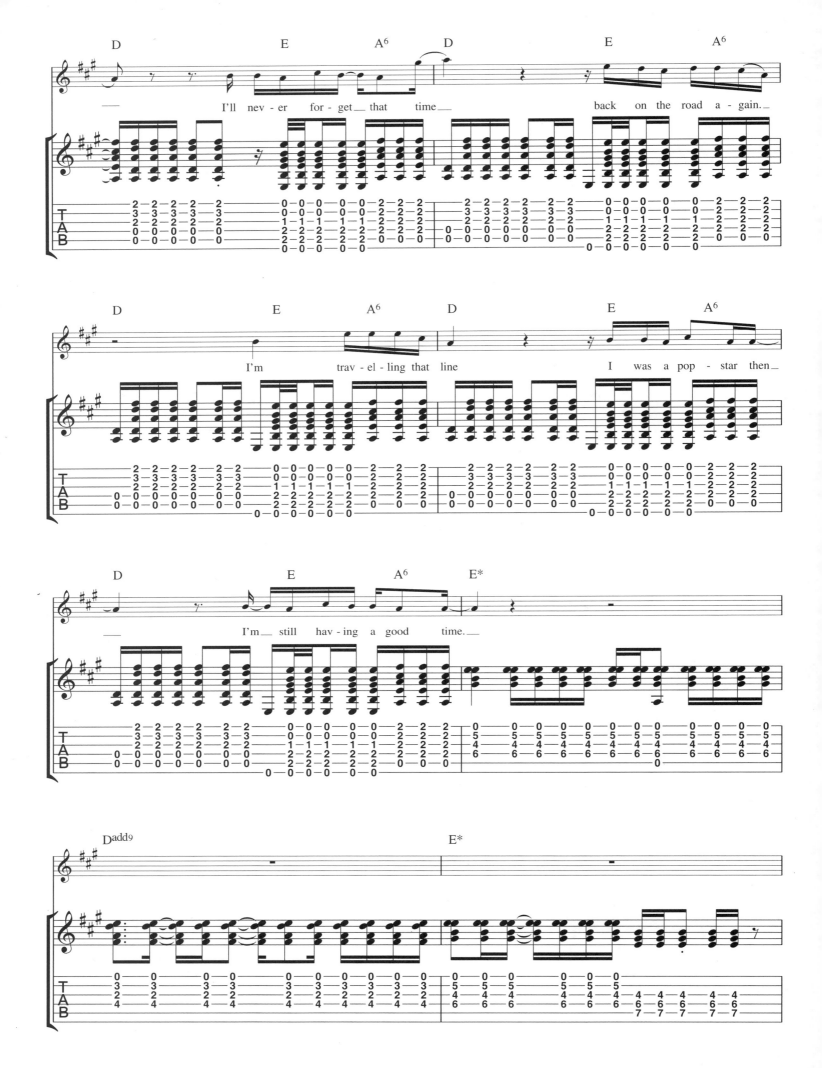

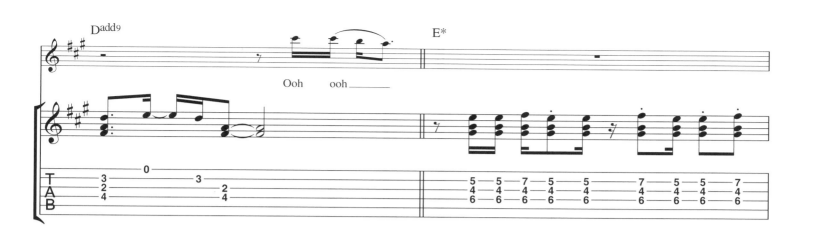

Ooh   ooh _____

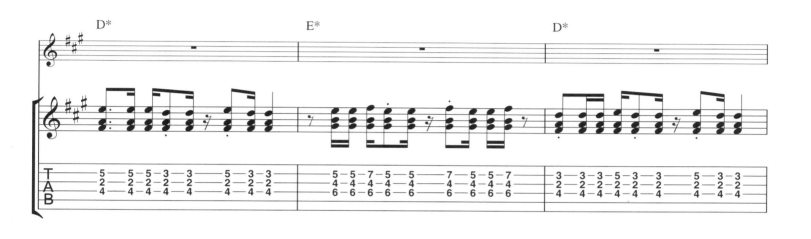

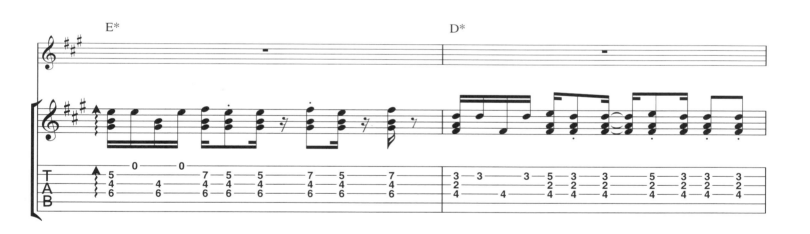

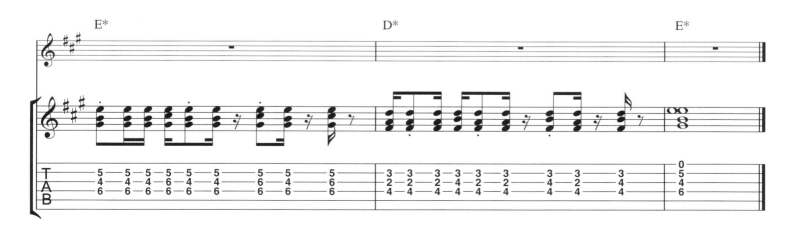

WHERE ARE YOU

WORDS & MUSIC BY CAT STEVENS

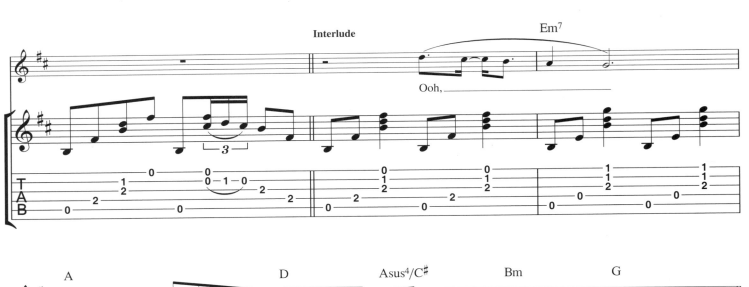

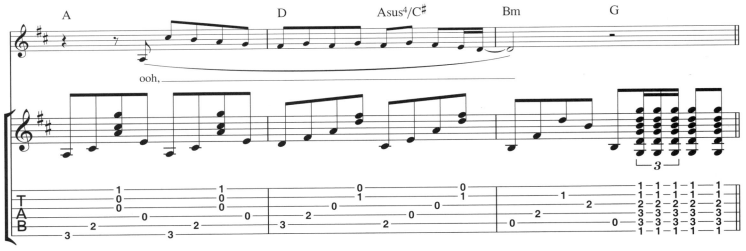

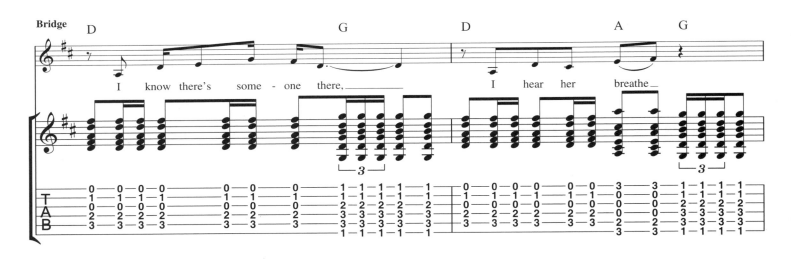

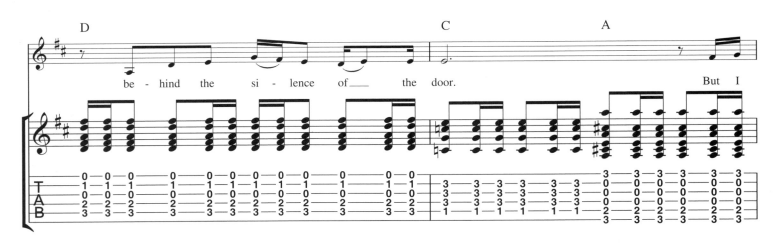

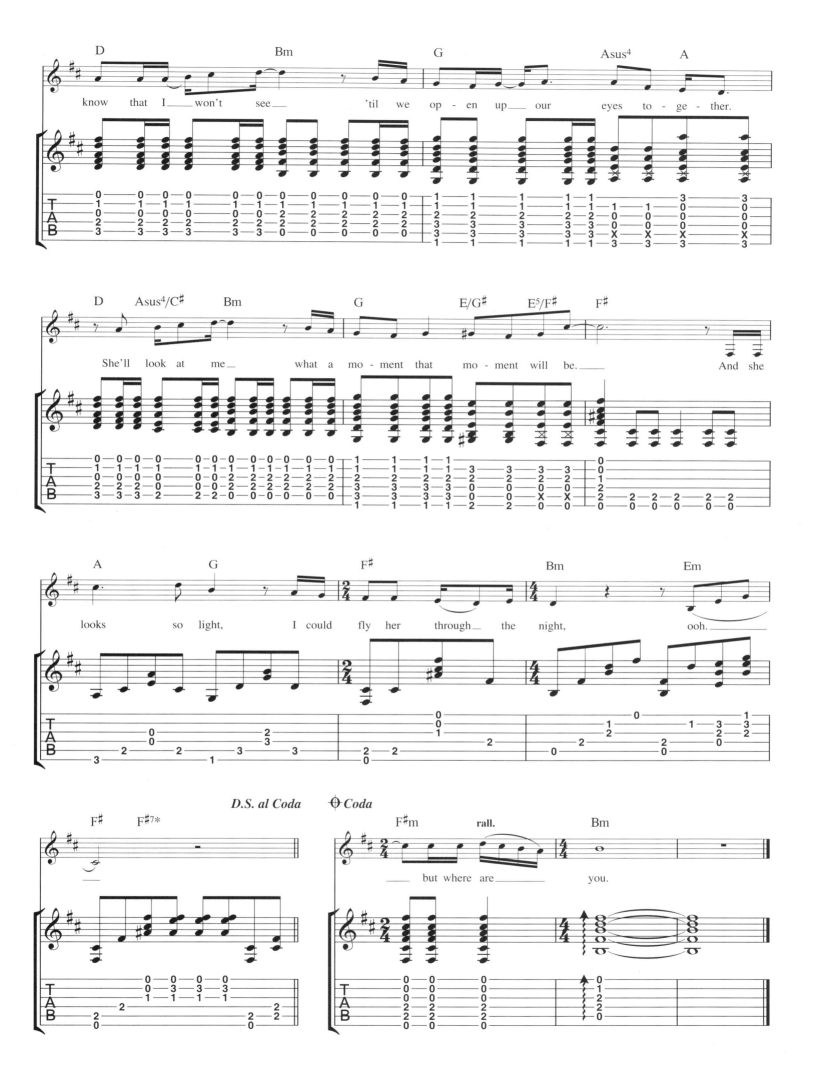

WHERE DO THE CHILDREN PLAY?

WORDS & MUSIC BY CAT STEVENS

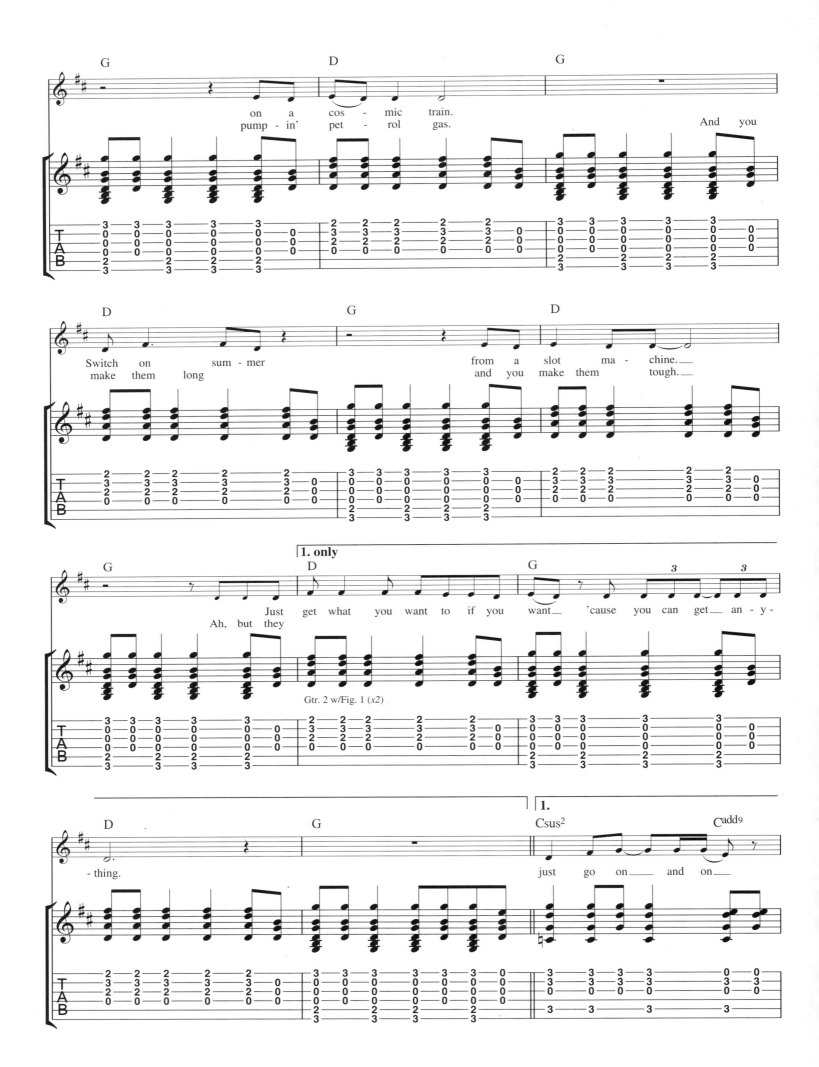

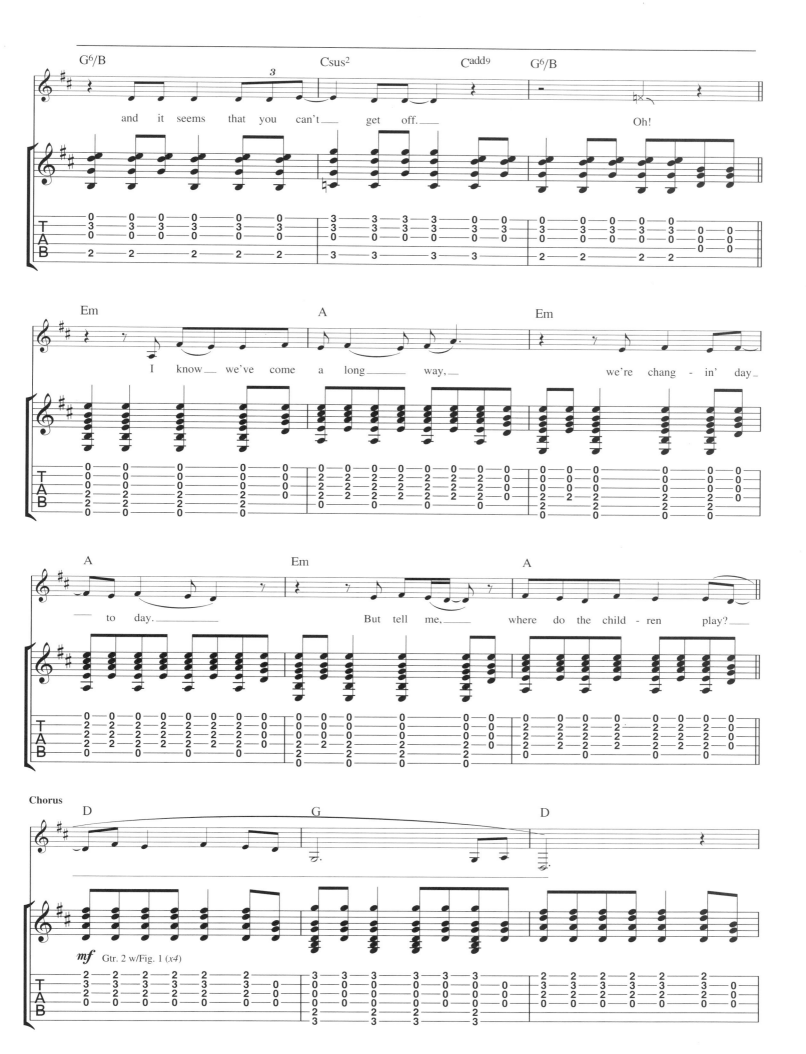

and it seems that you can't get off. Oh!

I know we've come a long way, we're chang - in' day to day. But tell me, where do the child - ren play?

Chorus

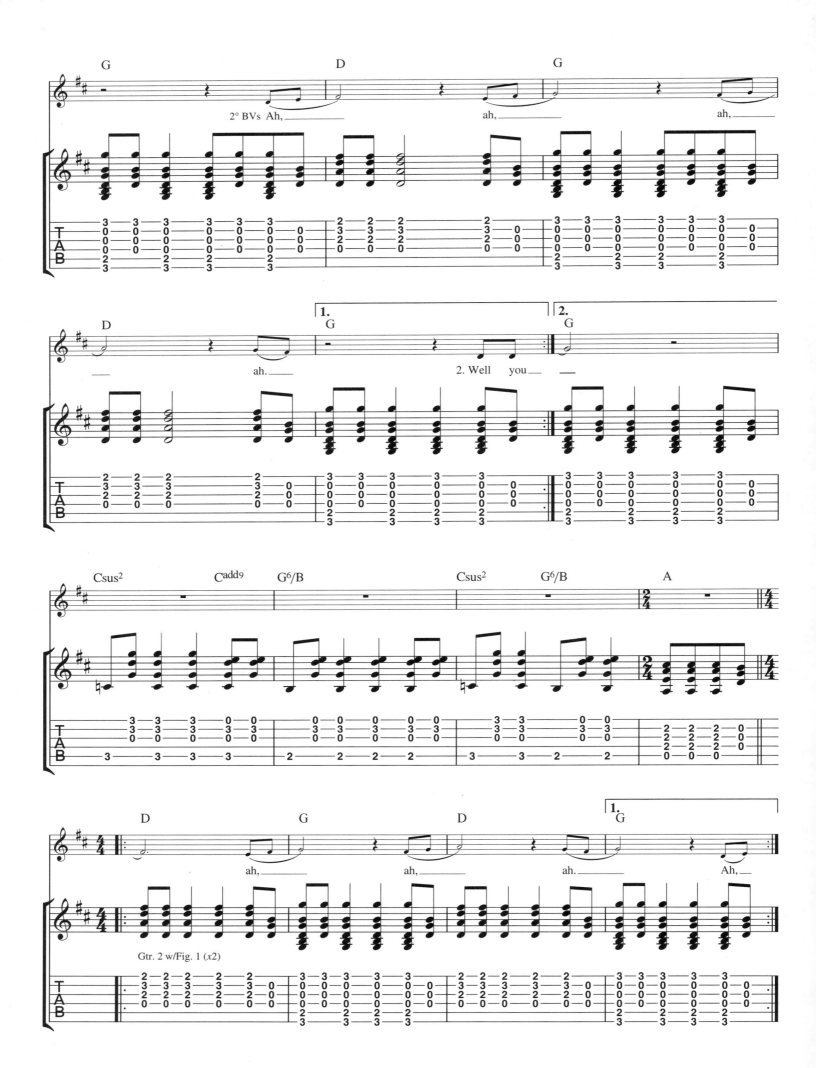

Outro chorus

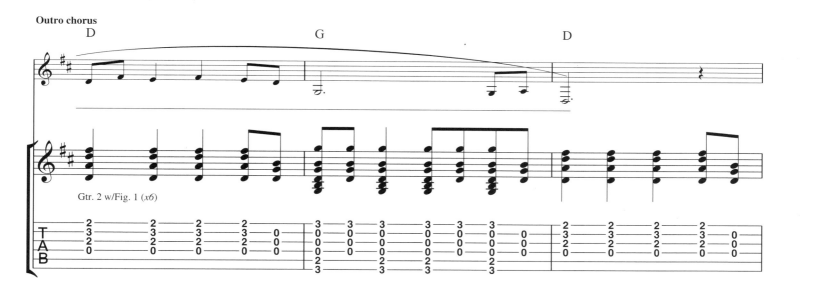

Gtr. 2 w/Fig. 1 (*x6*)

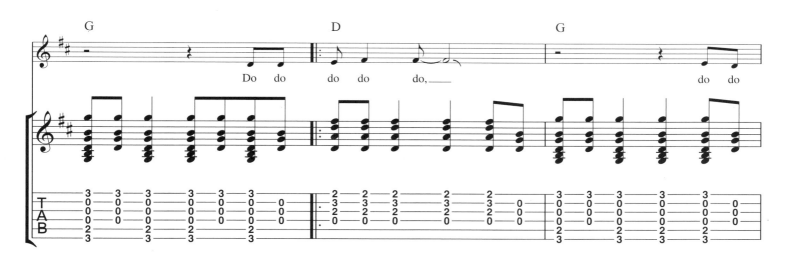

Do do do do do,_____ do do

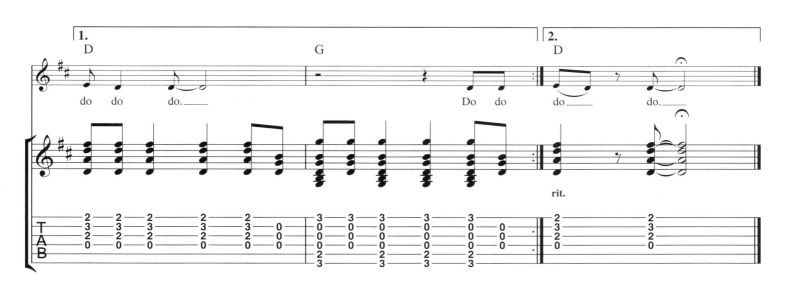

do do do._____ Do do do_____ do._____

rit.

WILD WORLD

WORDS & MUSIC BY CAT STEVENS

new_ and it's break-in' my heart_ your leav - in'. Ba - by I'm griev-in'.
two_ be - cause I nev - er wan-na see you sad girl. Don't be a bad_ girl.

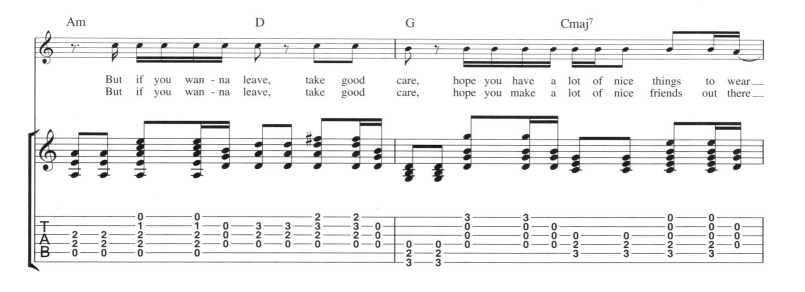

But if you wan - na leave, take good care, hope you have a lot of nice things to wear_
But if you wan - na leave, take good care, hope you make a lot of nice friends out there_

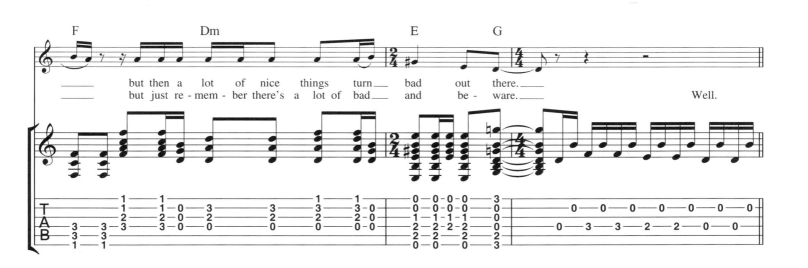

____ but then a lot of nice things turn_ bad out there.___
____ but just re - mem - ber there's a lot of bad_ and be - ware.___ Well.

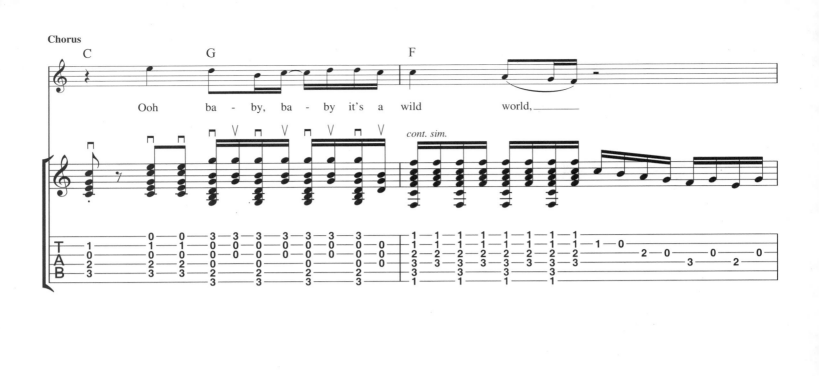

Ooh ba - by, ba - by it's a wild world,

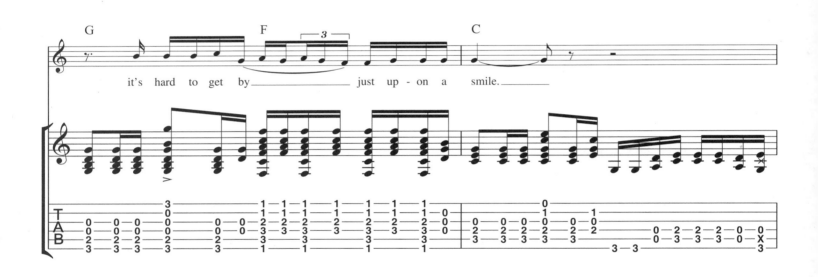

it's hard to get by _____ just up - on a smile. _____

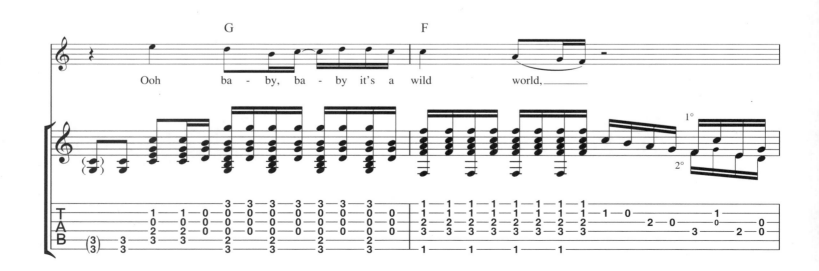

Ooh ba - by, ba - by it's a wild world,

care,___ hope you make a lot of nice friends___ out there.___ But just re - mem - ber there's a lot of bad

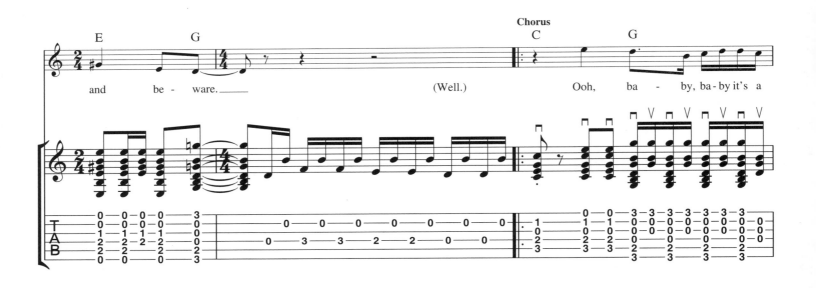

and be - ware.___ (Well.) Ooh, ba - by, ba - by it's a

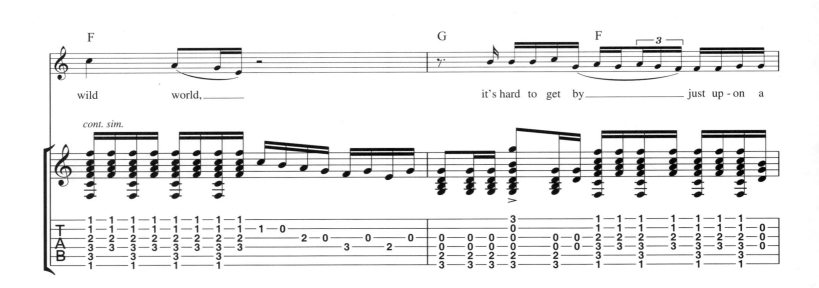

wild world,_____ it's hard to get by_____ just up - on a

smile.   Ooh,   ba - by, ba - by it's a

wild   world, _____   (And) I'll al - ways re - mem - ber you ___   like a

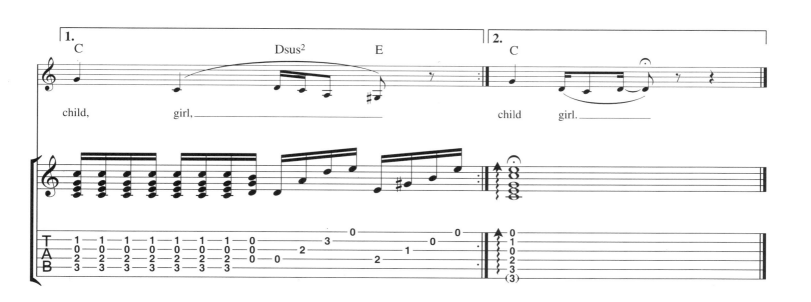

1.   **2.**

child,   girl, _____   child   girl. _____

THE WIND

WORDS & MUSIC BY CAT STEVENS

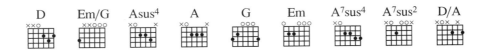

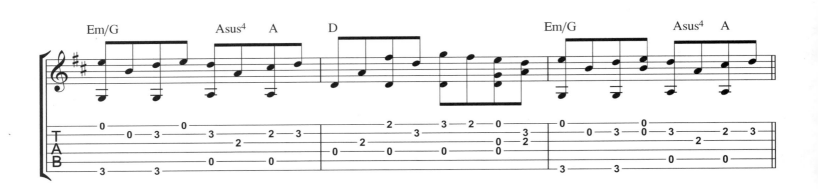

1. I lis- ten to the wind, to the wind of my soul,

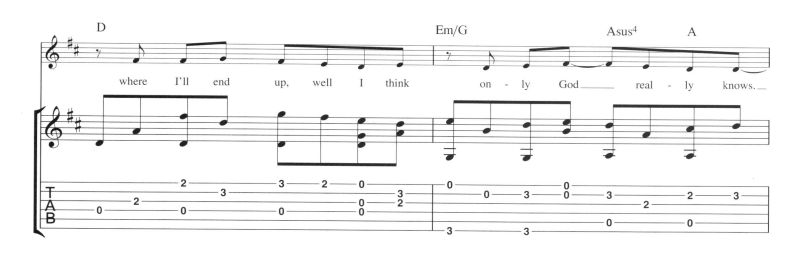

where I'll end up, well I think on - ly God ____ real - ly knows. ___

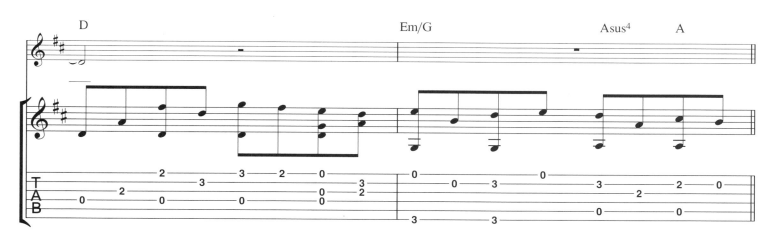

Chorus

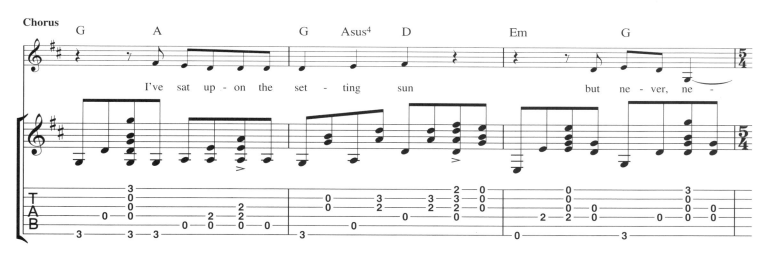

I've sat up - on the set - ting sun but ne - ver, ne -

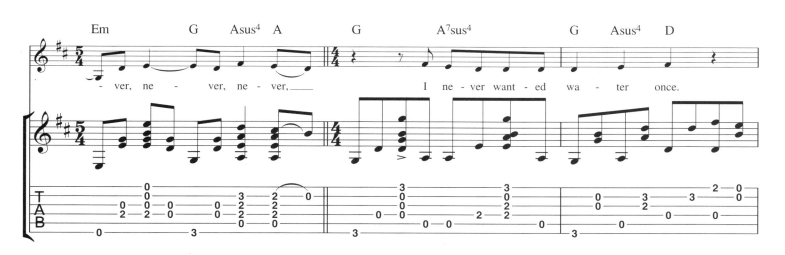

- ver, ne - ver, never, ____ I ne - ver want - ed wa - ter once.

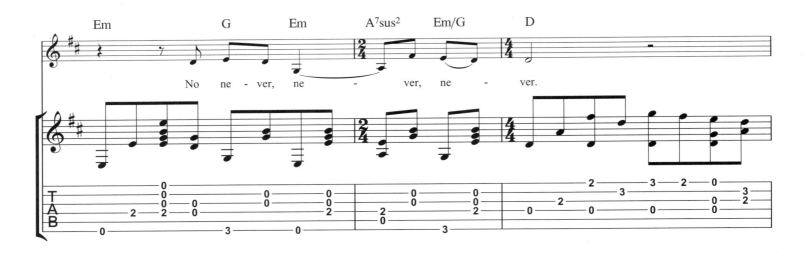

No ne - ver, ne - - ver, ne - ver.

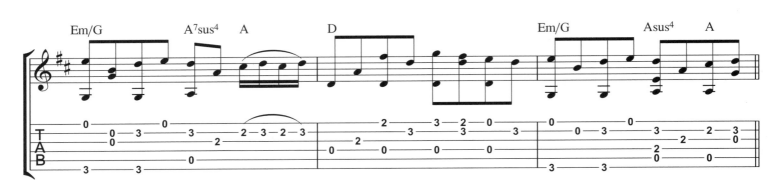

Verse

2. I list - en to my words but they fall far be - low,

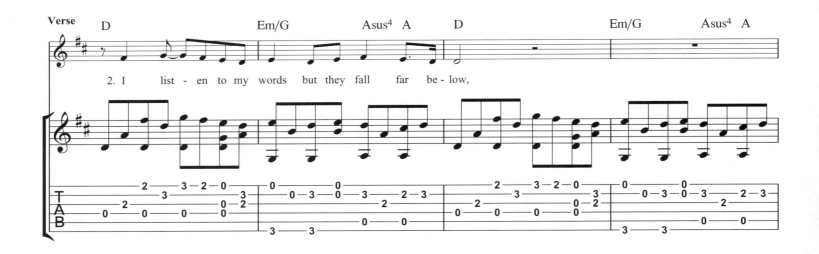

I let__ my mu - sic take me where my heart wants to go.

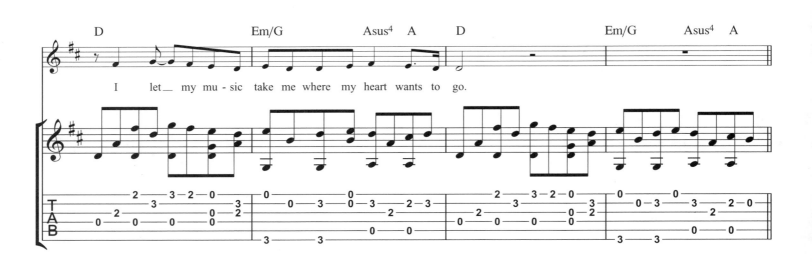

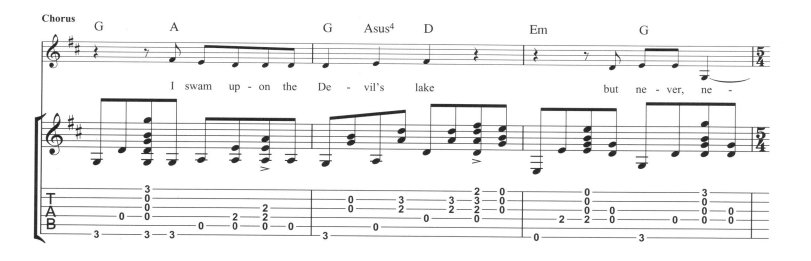

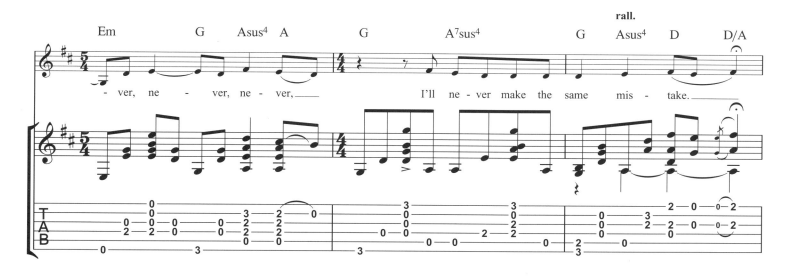

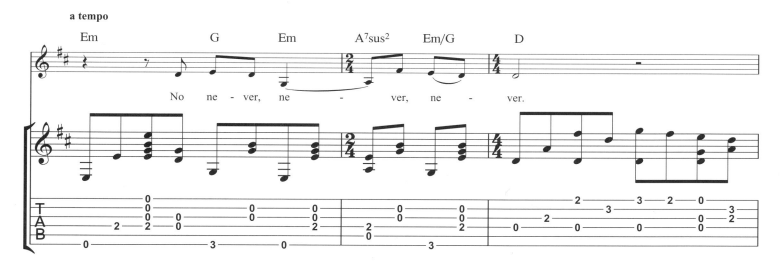

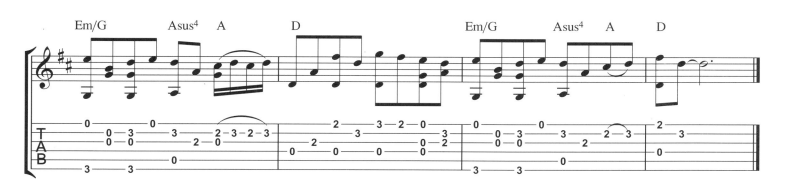

play *acoustic guitar with...*

Play guitar or sing along with the CD 'soundalike' backing tracks on all these great titles!

Every song in the music book is presented in easy-to-read guitar tablature with chord symbols and full lyrics

David Bowie *AM967109*

Eric Clapton *AM965954*

Bob Dylan *AM955999*

David Gray *AM970838*

Cat Stevens *AM976767*

Paul Simon *PS11469*

Simon & Garfunkel *PS11516*

20 Great Hits *AM976734*
Includes songs from Oasis, The Beatles,
Elvis Presley & The Who

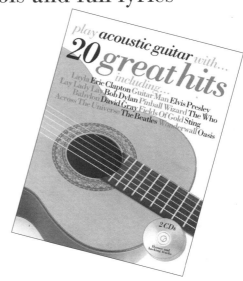